Bacon Orgazmia

Thomas F. Shubnell, Ph.D.

ISBN-13: 978-1515372929

ISBN-10: 1515372928

Cover and interior design by TFS

Back cover picture by John Meiers

Please ask your local library to carry my books.

Check my author page on Amazon for all my books.

We live in an interconnected world. Many are used to reading quickly, then going back and reading more background information later. I have included links within the text of this copious tome.

Links are easy enough to overlook while reading, but available for further in depth reading online. For eBook readers, the links are live for easy clicking.

Autohagiography

If you enjoy this, you will also love, "Gracious Me . . . Is Nothing Sacred." A non-sectarian and hilarious look at all religions from the beginning of time. It truly proves that laughter is good for the soul.

Medical humor abounds in the best selling "Medical Humor - medical nonsense to tickle your funnybone. A great collection of medical funny stuff, including stories, jokes, and hilarious pictures and cartoons.

"Unelectum All" is a reader's digest of politics. It makes the case for change using politicians own words. The book begins with early campaign promises and follows with political absurdities that have unfolded since then. This book needs to occupy the minds and bookshelves for 99% of voters.

A wacky book, "Men vs. Women, a Book of Lists" examines life from a different perspective and tells it all - the differences between the sexes are real and funny.

Even more fun can be found in "The Best of Terrible Tommy and Yucky Chucky," a collection of the best Terrible Tommy and Yucky Chucky jokes of all time.

More hilarious reading can be found in "Giggles, Gags, and Quips, Special Picks" a collection of the best jokes, pictures, billboards, stories, and cartoons.

Relationships can be funny, as shown in "Flowers, Foreplay, Facelifts, and Flatulence" a humorous romp through the four stages of relationships.

Also collect all the "Greatest Jokes of the Century" series of books. 25 wildly funny and hilarious compendiums of the greatest jokes, tidbits, stories, and trivia that are all sure to induce uncontrollable laughter.

"The Art of Installation and the Science of Implementation" is a serious project management primer, including tools and techniques for successful software implementation projects.

Don't forget to collect my Profound Thoughts, a 5 book series of great wisdom, aphorisms, and quotes from great minds.

Amazing Facts and Bite Sized Brain Food is a collection of thousands of amazing facts about the things you don't know, but want to know, and facts you think you know, but don't. Nestled in among the facts are bite sized tidbits of knowledge you can use to spice up any conversation.

All written by Thomas F. Shubnell and available online, your favorite bookstore, or as eBooks.

INTRODUCTION

"I had rather be shut up in a very modest cottage with my books, my family and a few old friends, dining on simple bacon, and letting the world roll on as it liked, than to occupy the most splendid post, which any human power can give." ~Thomas Jefferson

"There is no flavor comparable, I will contend, to that of the crisp, tawny, well-watched, not over-roasted, crackling, as it is well called - the very teeth are invited to their share of the pleasure at this banquet in overcoming the coy, brittle resistance - with the adhesive oleaginous - O call it not fat - but an indefinable sweetness growing up to it - the tender blossoming of fat - fat cropped in the bud - taken in the shoot - in the first innocence - the cream and quintessence of the child-pig's yet pure food - the lean, no lean, but a kind of animal manna - or, rather, fat and lean (if it must be so) so blended and running into each other, that both together make but one ambrosian result, or common substance." ~Charles Lamb

When it comes to the brain, there is almost no difference between bacon and an orgasm. Both affect the limbic system, which houses the pleasure center. This pleasure center and dopamine gives us the feeling of enjoyment and motivates us to obtain pleasure again. Dopamine is also the pleasure chemical that is delivered after eating delicious bacon or having an orgasm.

From early childhood, I have grown to become purveyor of propitious porcine pulchritude, piety, partiality, and passion. Some have even called me a bacon hedonist. This pandect of porcineology is my humble homage to the goodness and gallimaufry of all things bacon.

"Some books are to be tasted, others to be swallowed, and some few are to be chewed and digested." ~Sir Francis Bacon

This is one of the few...

Table of Contents

8

9

Bacon Thoughts

OVERVIEW

Throughout history, bacon has been an important staple of life. Dinosaurs did not eat bacon and now they are extinct.

Coincidence? *I think not.*

Humankind has evolved and has now arrived at the classic age of bacon. It is no longer a trend. It is no longer a fad. As of January, 2015, bacon's versatility has led it to continue its 10% per year increase in sales. After a dip in the 1980s, it was the turning point for Americans, and bacon was back on the forefront of everyone's minds. Bacon sales in the US have increased every year.

According to data from Statista, in 2012 a 19.6% (the largest share of the total) of US households reported having eaten two pounds of bacon in the previous thirty days. That rose to 20.8% in 2013 and 21.6% in 2014.

From early childhood, I have grown to become purveyor of porcine pulchritude, piety, partiality, and passion. I am a slave to my bacon mistress in the kitchen. Bacon is the fugacious food that makes other food taste better. It has become so popular that it is now even used as a condiment. It is the one meat that has converted more vegetarians back than any other. Even Kevin "Mo" Moreland, a vegetarian, made an exception to judge bacon at the Iowa Blue Ribbon Bacon Fest, Jan. 31, 2015. Bacon has become the truffle of America, indeed the world.

Nutritionists struggled for years to come up with a name for the fifth taste sensation to describe savory in addition to sweet, sour, bitter, and salty. They finally chose umami, because they thought bacon did not sound scientific enough. Update: They are still trying. During February 2015, researchers from Deakin University in Australia published a paper in the journal Flavor arguing that, "the next 5 to 10 years should reveal, conclusively whether fat can be classified as the sixth taste."

There are five criteria that need to be met to call something a primary taste. It starts with chemical stimuli, such as salt which then trigger specific receptors on taste buds. There has to be a viable a pathway between the receptors and the brain, and it must be able to perceive and process the taste. The whole process needs to trigger downstream effects in the body. *That could almost be the definition of bacon!*

A TIMELINE

The pig dates back over 40 million years to fossils which indicate that wild porcine animals roamed forests and swamps in Europe and Asia. Remains of the earliest known North American Perchoerus (pecarry), are from sediments dating from 37 million years ago in North America.

From 35,000 to 20,000 BC, boars, as well as other sacred animals are painted in realistic fashion by humans on rock faces and cave interiors throughout Ice Age Europe. From 11,000 to 9000 BC, pigs are first domesticated in central Asia, southern Turkey and Iran. from 5500–4500 BC, the first domesticated pigs appear in Europe. These are a result of successful breeding of Near Eastern domesticated pigs with the European wild boar. During 4000 BC, the Emperor of China gives pork "royal status" when he decreed that the Chinese people must raise and breed hogs.

The Romans improved pig breeding and spread pork production throughout their empire. Two main types were developed: one breed was large, with floppy ears, and produced copious amounts of lard, while the other was of a smaller frame, with erect ears, used primarily for meat.

The word we use derives originally from the Old High German bacho, meaning "buttock", which derived from the Proto-Germanic backoz, meaning 'back', in Old Dutch they called it *baken*.

By the 14th century, it became known in Old French as 'bacun', meaning 'back meat'.

It was a staple dish throughout Europe and Christopher Columbus brought, among other things, pigs with him to the Americas.

An offshoot of the name, 'buccaneers' of the Caribbean derived their name from the Arawak Indian word buccan, referring to a wooden frame used for smoking meats. The French changed this to boucan and called the French hunters who used these frames to cook and preserve feral cattle and the offspring of Columbus' pigs on the island of Hispaniola boucanier. English colonists anglicized the word to buccaneers.

Hernando de Soto was the true father of the American pork industry. He brought America's first 13 pigs to Tampa Bay, Fla., in 1539. As the herds grew, explorers used the pigs not only for eating as fresh meat, but for salt pork, and preserved pork. American Indians were reportedly so fond of the taste of pork that attacks to acquire it resulted in some of the worst assaults on the expedition. By the time Hernando died, his original herd of 13 pigs had grown to 700.

Until well into the sixteenth century, bacon or bacoun was a Middle English term. What the English were historically calling bacon at the time referred to a specific cut of pork belly and pork loin and mostly cut from breeds of pig that had been specifically bred to make what we now call 'back bacon'. The term bacon also comes from various Germanic and French dialects. It derives from the French bako, Common Germanic bakkon and Old Teutonic backe, all of which refer to the back. Although etymologists argue over its specific origin, each area had its own name and fondness for this remarkable and wonderful food.

In Ebenezer Cooke's 1708 poem The Sot-Weed Factor, a satire of life in early colonial America, the narrator complained that practically all the food in America was bacon-infused.

Up to the end of the 18th century, the way bacon was dry-cured and produced was notably different from the way is was done during the 19th Century. Using the dry-cure method, bacon is cut and rubbed with salt by hand before being cured and then smoked. Although during the 1700s, John Harris opened the world's first commercial bacon processing plant in Wiltshire, England a place considered by some to be the bacon capital of the world and helped develop another method by curing 1/2 pork sides in a brine curing solution, a method which became known as the "Wiltshire Cure." His company, C&T Harris (Calne) Ltd., continued operations until 1983.

The meat became more popular in the United States in 1924, when cold cut production company Oscar Mayer introduced packages of pre-sliced bacon for sale (See Breakfast, Bacon, and Bernays).

Google Trends shows the rise in popularity of bacon in headlines from 2004 forward. The interest in bacon spread from England, US, and Australia throughout the rest of the world to the phenomenon it enjoys currently. Although bacon may have achieved meme status via the internet, it has been a meme long before the internet was invented.

In this health-conscious day and age, you would think that bacon would be low on the list of preferred foods due to its fat content. Yet, as anyone who dabbles in bacon knows, bacon is solely responsible for giving a boost to the pork market. Bacon is so popular as a sandwich ingredient and a favorite of chefs in fine dining establishments that bacon shortages have caused prices to soar. However, bacon is still a bargain that cannot be beat when it comes to adding flavor.

During recent years many have been calling it 'nature's candy' or 'meat candy'.

The Adkins diet helped show that bacon can be used by people trying to lose weight.

People have been eating bacon cheeseburgers for many years, but new recipes call for mixing the meat with bacon before cooking.

Bacon peanut butter sandwiches are becoming common breakfast items. *(I predict that peanut butter will become the 'new bacon', but not in the foreseeable future.)*

The Seattle Weekly cites the origin of the blog, Bacon Unwrapped, in 2005. Boston hosted a bacon eating contest in 2007 and many cities have since followed suit. (see Bacon Events later in this book) During 2008, the LA Times produce an article titled, '1001 things to do with bacon' and listed things from martinis to full meals.

The online recipe for 'bacon explosion', forming bacon weave to wrap a filling of spiced sausage and crumbled bacon appeared to continue the online devotion to all things bacon. It was followed, using the bacon weave to inspire many more sumptuous recipes, including one of my favorites, bacon cheese sandwich, made with two bacon weaves and cheese in the middle.

Bacon was included in the first meal consumed on the moon by Neil Armstrong and Buzz Aldrin.

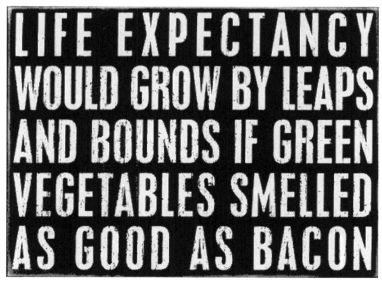

LIFE EXPECTANCY WOULD GROW BY LEAPS AND BOUNDS IF GREEN VEGETABLES SMELLED AS GOOD AS BACON

Fancy Dress Ball Award

The Author in Fancy Dress as a Side of Bacon, designed by himself, which took the First Prize of Forty Guineas at the Covent Garden Fancy Dress Ball, April 1894.

(PS – that is a different author, not the author of this book)

Share a rasher of bacon love with your BFF

THE SANITARY PIGGERY

"Cleanliness is next to Godliness. The Hog is naturally much more cleanly in its habits than many of those who say he isn't." William Emerson Baker

The Ridge Hill Farms, Needham, MA was an 800 acre farm developed by Baker.

In June of 1875, Baker threw a huge party to celebrate the laying of the cornerstone for his new Sanitary Piggery. 2,500 invited guests attended the event, including Governor Gaston of Massachusetts, Mayor Cobb of Boston, State senators and representatives, generals, members of foreign legations, and delegations of the 5th Maryland Regiment, the South Carolina Light Infantry, and the 5th Massachusetts Regiment.

In the Sanitary Piggery, the pigs were kept in strictly clean conditions and given wholesome food. It was even rumored that the residents were provided with little beds and little silk sheets in keeping with Baker's sense of humor.

Baker believed that the usual method of pig-keeping, penned in filthy sties or allowed to roam free and eat trash, bred diseased animals with tainted meat: "The flesh of those swine fed on city garbage is liable to be unfit for market, as this garbage is often fermented and sour. Thus the City of Boston, by the disposition of its garbage, directly aids in filling our hospital wards with patients diseased from eating unwholesome pork."

"I like pigs. Dogs look up to us. Cats look down on us. Pigs treat us as equals." ~Winston Churchill

"Thou shall not kill. Thou shall not commit adultery. Don't eat pork. I'm sorry, what was that last one?? Don't eat pork. God has spoken. Is that the word of God or is that pigs trying to outsmart everybody?" ~ Jon Stewart

BACON ASSIGNMENT

shot sentences
a. I like bacon.
b. You like bacon.
c. We like bacon.
compound sentences
a. I like bacon very much, so I eat bacon.
b. You like bacon a lot, so you eat bacon.
c. We like bacon so much, so we eat bacon.
Subject First
a. Bacon is so amazing.
b. Bacon is very crispy.
c. Bacon is very steamy.
Adjectives first
a. Crispy bacon in my mouth.
b. Amazing bacon in my mouth.
c. Tasty bacon on a plate.
Adverbs First
a. Quickly I chewed and swallowed the bacon
b. Quietly I devoured all the bacon.
c. Happily I ate every single strip of bac

One of my 6th grade students just earned an A for the year

more awesome pictures at THEMETAPICTURE.COM

BACON WEDDINGS

A June 2013 Wedding was held for a couple who bonded over a shared love for Puerto Rican pork shoulder at the San Diego County Fair among a full day of bacon-themed events. Adrienne Dunvan and Eddie Quinones were the winners of a contest to get married during the "Big Bite Bacon Fest" at the fair.

Jesse Lozano, a local DJ presided over the nuptials.

Onlookers and the bacon-clad wedding party showered the newlyweds with bacon bits as they took their first steps as husband and wife. The Donut Bar provided an oversized maple donut sprinkled with bacon for a wedding cake.

A honeymoon was planned in a Baltimore neighborhood known as the Pigtown Historic District to attend the 12th Annual Pigtown Festival.

The Big Bite Bacon Fest features tastings of bacon-infused dishes, craft beers from local breweries, live entertainment and a Big Daddy Bacon Pageant.

* * *

"We wanted something different and neither one of us is really very big on cookies," he said. "It seems that every wedding you go to, everyone always ends up taking home a box of cookies at the end of the night that they take into the office on Monday."

The couple had attended an event where one of the dessert items was chocolate-covered bacon, and that got them thinking.

"It was fantastic and we thought, 'Why not?'" he said.

The two of them love bacon, like most people. They suggested the bacon table to their caterer at Leo's Ristorante in Howland, Ohio, near the bride's hometown of Niles.

"We will have a rosemary-flavored bacon, a jerked version, and then a pie-spiced bacon and a chocolate-covered bacon to honor the sweet dessert tradition."

CHURCHES OF BACON

It is well known that pious people prefer pork, even Jewish people call it the 'sizzling scent of sin'.

The **Holy Church of Bacon** promotes consumption of, and unfaltering love for, the holiest of holy foods: Bacon.

These were part of the salty scrolls translated by a scholarly team of the Bacon Baron and Lord Bacon of Sizzlingham, their work was overseen by his holiness the Bacon Bishop of Porkland.

1 Thou shalt not consider Bacon on the same level as any other food, as it is above all.
2 Thou shalt not consume imitation Bacon.
3 Thou shalt not stop pursuing Baconlightenment until it is reached.
4 Thou shalt not forget to consume Bacon for ten days.
5 Thou shalt spread the word of Bacon to all.

* * *

The **United Church of Bacon** began as a feud with another church, whose members were illegally parking.

Its Tenets of Baconism begin with: "In the beginning there was the Big Bang, which begat all of time and space. Eventually sacrificial pigs evolved and the god of bacon did come to be." Its first Goal of Baconism, as part of its mission is to: "Praise Bacon!"

* * *

Pinterest has a Church of Bacon

* * *

There is also the **Official Church of Baconology**

Baconology is a fellowship of bacon consumers. Everyone who loves to eat bacon is welcome to join the **Church of Baconology** and become a Baconologist.

* * *

Ministry of Bacon (*old site, but still interesting*)

* * *

Twitter has Pastor Porky @**Church_Of_Bacon** - Guiding the lost in the worship of our Savior, Bacon. It is the embodiment of harmony between good and evil.

Twitter also has @**BaconRapt** - One should never become lax on the quality of bacon they purchase.

* * *

Google+ the **Church of Bacon** – see above

* * *

Facebook includes many devotees of bacon

The **Official Church of Baconology**, also see above.

* * *

Brotherhood of Bacon web site

* * *

Church and Country of Anti-Bacon - Since Saudi Arabia operates under Islamic law, all food entering the country must be 'halal'. It is a country that considers all its citizens to be Muslim and any non-Muslim expats must abide by its strict rules. Furthermore, because Saudi Arabia contains the two holy mosques, it considers having any pork inside the country a desecration.

In addition, none of the bacon religions would be allowed there. It is against the law for non-Muslims to worship in public in Saudi Arabia and there are no houses of worship to cater to non-Muslims. It would be blasphemous for churches or other places of worship to exist there.

Some ethnic religions have been known to keep kosher, except for bacon.

PATRON SAINT OF BACON

St Anthony the Great, also referred to as 'the Abbott' was an Egyptian Christian in the pre-Islamic period that lived in the desert as a religious hermit for part of his life.

Swineherds took Anthony as their patron, and he thus became the patron saint of pork butchers and also the patron saint of bacon.

During his lifetime, skin diseases were sometimes treated with applications of pork fat, which reduced inflammation and itching. He is also the patron saint of epilepsy, amputees, shingles, gravediggers, hermits, lost items, and Canas Brazil.

Because Anthony's intervention aided in the same conditions, he was often shown in art accompanied by a pig. A person who saw the art work, but did not have it explained, thought there was a direct connection between Anthony and pigs. People who worked with swine took him as their patron.

He was born 251 at Heracleus, Egypt and died 356 at Mount Colzim of natural causes.

CHINESE HOROSCOPE AND PIGS

Half of all the pigs in the world live in China. The pig is the last of the 12 animals in the Chinese zodiac. The pig is seen to represent, fortune, honesty, happiness, fertility, and virility.

The Pig is an enlightening personality blessed with patience and understanding. People born under the sign of the Pig enjoy life and all it has to offer. They are honest and thoughtful and expect the same of other people. Pigs can be perceived as oblivious or gullible, because they care about others so much that they will do just about anything for a friend in need.

Characteristics: Hardworking, Giving, Willing, Helpful, Materialistic, Gullible, Oblivious, Obstinate.

The characteristics of the Pig Sign are tempered by one of the five Chinese elements of metal, water, wood, fire, and earth overlaying a 5-year cycle of characteristics on the original 12-year cycle.

Year of the Pig: Pig Years recur every twelfth year. The Chinese New Year does not fall on a specific date. 18 February 2007 - 6 February 2008: Fire Pig, 5 February 2019 - 24 January 2020: Earth Pig.

People born in the Year of the Pig share certain characteristics. The Pig Sign is an abbreviated way of characterizing that individual's personality. Following are features associated with the Sign of the Pig.

Twelfth in order, Chinese name ZHU, sign of honesty

Western Counterpart, Scorpio

Fire Pig 2007 - Active, outgoing and extroverted, Fire Pigs breathe new life into everything they do. These Pigs are vivid, motivated individuals who cannot be deterred from a goal once they have set it. They are emotional and passionate about their loved ones, their occupations and their objectives. They are bold and vivacious, unafraid to take risks despite the consequences. Do not double-cross a Fire Pig. They have the ability to be quite abrasive when things do not turn out as they planned.

Earth Pig 2019 - Laid back and reliable, Earth Pigs are at their happiest at home with their families. They are organized and pragmatic, preparing a strategy for every project they take on. They are fruitful at work and are content being one of the employees.

Pigs at Work - Pigs generally do really well when they get to be creative. They usually do better at jobs where they can express themselves. They are enthusiastic about taking on new responsibility at work and jump in to give a hand to colleagues in need. Pigs are well-liked by co-workers, because are so willing to help and they have an eye for detail that makes them quite invaluable to upper management.

Pigs and Money - Pigs love to spend money. Pigs have a knack for being able to find a diamond in the rough. Although they can sometimes be thrifty with money, most of the time it is the reverse.

Pigs have been at the centre of Chinese culture, cuisine and family life for thousands of years. Pork is the country's essential meat. In Mandarin the word for "meat" and "pork" are the same. The character for "family" is a pig under a roof.

Between 1975 and 2013, Chinese pork consumption grew an average of 5.7 percent per year compared to an average yearly rate of 1.3 percent in the US. Differences in growth rates caused Chinese consumption to be over 6 times larger than US consumption in 2013 - 54 million tons in China compared to 8.6 million tons in the US.

Even though it raises almost half the pigs in the world, China became a net importer of pork in 2008. It has imported approximately 400,000 tons of pork per year in recent years.

Bacon is not the Chuck Norris of food.
Chuck Norris is the bacon of people.

FATHER AND SON

Some folks just like to keep it in the family.

PIG FACTS

- Pigs are mammals and originated from Eurasian wild boars (Sus scrofa). Pigs belong to the family Suidae, which includes the warthog (Phacochoerus) and bushpig (Potamochoerus) of Africa, the babirusa (Babyrousa) of Indonesia.

- Wild boar and pigs are found on every continent except Antarctica.

- Although selective breeding by the pig industry has altered the appearance and physiology of domestic pigs, comparative studies show that their behavioral characteristics are fundamentally the same as those of the wild boar.

- Pigs are part of the order Artiodactyla, or even-toed ungulates. They share this order with cattle, sheep, goats, camels, deer, giraffes and hippopotami.

- Pigs have been domesticated since approximately 5,000 to 7,000 years ago.

- In Great Britain the Yorkshire and Tamworth pig breeds are bred specifically for bacon and referred to as bacon breeds.

- The largest pig ever recorded was a Poland-China hog, named 'Big Bill'. Owned by Burford Butler of Jackson Tennessee in 1933, this huge pig weighed 2,552 lbs and had a height of five feet and a length of nine feet. His stomach was so big it dragged on the ground. (A friend, Tom Knudson, won an award in Kansas for his prized Poland-China hog.)

- Pig, also called hog or swine, is a generic term for all pigs regardless of gender or breed.

- A male pig is called a boar. A female pig, before she has piglets is called a gilt, after a sow.

- There are approximately two billion pigs worldwide, including boars.

- A pig is more intelligent than a dog and ranks fourth in intelligence behind chimpanzees, dolphins, and elephants. They are curious and insightful animals who are widely accepted as being smarter than young children of at least 3 years of age.

- A pig's orgasm lasts thirty minutes. *Wow, that's makin' some bacon!*

- Some pigs have straight and some have curly tails.

- Contrary to popular belief, pigs are clean creatures. A clean pig has about the same amount of body odor as a clean human being. Pigs defecate away from their living areas. Piglets will leave the nest to relieve themselves when they are only a few hours old.

- Adult pigs can run at speeds of up to 11 miles an hour.

- Pigs bred for bacon production are known as *baconers* and are sold at an age of around 24 weeks. They have a higher body fat ratio and are typically heavier than other pigs.

- Pigs bred for pork come in three grades; *porkers, superporkers,* and *finishers*. These tend to have lean meat and are smaller than baconers.

- Pigs prefer to eat slowly and savor their food.

- In 1993, the 590,000 sows and 10 million top hogs in the state of North Carolina produced 9 million tons of fresh manure, enough to annually provide all the fertilizer needs for the state's six largest agricultural counties.

- A mature pig has 44 teeth.

- National Pig Carvers Association - The actual date when pig decoys were first employed in the hunt for the wild pig is not known.

- Pigs are not always pink they can be red as well as black and white.

- Pigs are extremely social animals. They form close bonds with other individuals and love close contact and lying down together.

- Pigs are peaceful animals, rarely showing aggression. The exception, as with many animals, is when a mother with her young offspring is provoked or threatened.

- Wild pigs play an important role in managing ecosystems and maintaining biodiversity. By rooting, and thus disturbing the soil, they create areas for new plant colonization. They also spread fruit plants by dispersing their seeds.

- Pigs have a tremendous sense of smell. The large round disk of cartilage at the tip of the snout is connected to muscle that gives it extra flexibility and strength for rooting in the ground.

- Pigs are great swimmers.

- Pigs snuggle close to one another and prefer to sleep nose to nose. They dream, much as humans do. In their natural surroundings, pigs spend hours playing, sunbathing, and exploring. Pigs enjoy listening to music, playing with soccer balls, and getting massages.

- Pigs communicate constantly with one another. More than 20 vocalizations have been identified that pigs use in different situations, from wooing mates to express hunger. Pigs greet one another vociferously and by making contact with their snouts. While foraging or exploring, they stay in contact through constant vocalization and are always aware of each other's actions, often learning by watching others' behavior.

- Their large, pricked ears act like radar dishes and can localize sound to a threshold of just 4 degrees, making them one of the most accurate localizers of sound in the animal kingdom. They can distinguish between very subtle differences in tone and are known to use vocal noises to communicate during feeding, courtship, exploring, and other social activities.

- Pigs appear to have a good sense of direction and have found their way home over great distances.

- The average lifespan of wild boars and feral pigs is about 4 years. Other pigs live on average about fifteen years.

- Pigs eyes are placed on both sides of their head, so they have a wide field of vision.

- Pigs raised for meat in North America are usually slaughtered at about 6 months of age.

- Pigs have been observed to work in collaboration to free themselves from their pens.

- Pigs are widely known to be highly inquisitive, with considerable learning and problem-solving abilities. They easily learn to operate levers and switches to obtain food and water, and to adjust ambient temperature.

- After teaching pigs to control a special joystick with their snouts, researchers at Pennsylvania State University found that pigs could learn to play simple matching games by moving the cursor around a computer screen. The pigs demonstrated a similar capacity as primates for learning the tasks.

- Pigs have the largest repertoire of functional olfactory receptor genes of any mammal sequenced to date.

- Guinea pigs are neither pigs nor from Guinea.

- Experts have determined that the average pig squeals at a level of 100-115 decibels. A jet's engine only reaches about 112 decibels at takeoff. *Bacon does not squeal, it sizzles.*

- China raises more pigs than the next 43 pig growing countries combined.

Pig History

Pigs were first domesticated in Europe and Asia approximately 10,000 years ago.

Polynesians may have introduced domestic pigs to Hawaii sometime during the first millennium. It is generally believed that when Christopher Columbus landed in Cuba in 1493, he brought to North America the first domestic pigs, which subsequently spread throughout the Caribbean.

In 1539, the Spanish explorers brought the first pigs to the mainland when they settled in Florida. The pigs were released into the wild and they spread throughout the region that is now the southeastern United States. Throughout the 17th and 18th centuries, the colonists brought pigs to America and raised them as free-roaming animals. Those who escaped into the wild became feral.

During the 20th century, European wild boars were brought to the United States as a game animal for hunting. Some of these animals escaped and mated with free-ranging domestic and feral pigs. Today's feral pigs are a combination of descendents of escaped farmed pigs, wild boar, and hybrids of the two.

Several centuries ago, the wild boar became extinct in Britain as a result of hunting and habitat destruction, but they have since been reintroduced and are thriving. Great Britain produces bacon using breeds of pig that have a regionally unique genetic lineage and in Europe almost of all the well established national pig breeds are genetically descended from the same European boar which is genetically different from the Asian or American boar.

Feral pigs and wild boar live in a wide range of habitats, but primarily dwell in forests and woodlands, where trees and vegetation provide shelter and supplies of their preferred foods, acorns and beechnuts. They dig out beds under the cover of oak trees and shrubs, and prefer swamps, marshes, and other areas with year-round access to surface water and moist ground for wallowing.

Pigs are halfway between carnivores and plant-eaters. Pigs subsist primarily on plant matter, but they are omnivores and supplement their diets with earthworms, insects, amphibians, reptiles, rodents, and carrion.

Like a cat's whiskers, a pig's snout provides the animal with heightened senses to navigate and interact with the environment. Under natural conditions, pigs may spend 75% of their daily activity engaged in rooting and foraging.

The nasal disc on a pig's snout, while rigid enough to be used for digging, has numerous sensory receptors for a well-developed sense of smell. Pigs can smell roots and tubers that are deep underground.

Pigs can also use odor from urine and the facial glands to identify other pigs, and even pigs that are unable to see are able to recognize other individuals in their group.

Pigs also communicate by scent-marking prominent features in their home ranges. They are not very territorial, and the purpose of scent-marking is to establish group cohesion, rather than to just mark territory.

They regularly bathe in water and wallow in mud in order to prevent heat stress, much like elephants. Pigs do not have sweat glands, so the mud covering their bodies offers thermoregulatory protection, protection from flies, and helps to prevent sunburn.

Pigs stay cool during warmer months by limiting most of their activity to night, and being primarily nocturnal also helps them to avoid predators.

Pigs instinctively huddle together to stay warm as young piglets and throughout adulthood.

Pig Birth

Gilts (young female pigs) reach puberty at 5-8 months of age. European wild boars typically begin breeding when they are 18-20 months old and normally produce one litter per year. The gestation period is 114 days.

A sow can give birth to a litter containing 7 to 12 piglets, about twice a year. The average litter is 12 piglets. The largest litter of pigs on record is 37.

A baby pig, or piglet, weighs about 1.5 kilograms at birth and will double its weight in seven days.

Weaning occurs at three months of age, but young pigs continue to live with their mothers. Two or more sows usually join together in an extended family.

Newborn piglets learn to run to their mothers' voices and to recognize their own names. Mother pigs sing to their young while nursing.

The young are well-developed at birth, or precocial, which is rare among polytocous mammals. They are among the most precocious newborns of all ungulate species, but share the delicate metabolisms and weak constitutions of the polytocous mammals. They can see and hear at birth, and start to walk within a few minutes of being born.

Piglets quickly find their mother's teats to nurse, often with some gentle nudging and encouragement from the sow. A teat order, the beginning stage of social organization in the life of a pig, is formed on the first day, giving each piglet his or her own specific teat for the rest of the nursing period.

The sow and her piglets use various vocalizations to initiate nursing, and newborn piglets will recognize and respond to their mother's voice when she calls them to suckle. Piglets can distinguish between their own mother's voice and that of other sows.

While the sow stays in the nest with her litter, isolated from the sounder (group of pigs) for about 1-2 weeks, she is very protective, and this period of exclusive contact with her piglets enables the development of strong bonds. One or two days after giving birth, the sow begins to leave on short foraging trips, though staying close to the nest and her young.

Exploratory behavior, such as rooting, develops within the first few days of life, and the piglets soon begin to follow the sow on short excursions away from the nest. When separated from their mother, piglets call her with distinctive vocalizations, and the sow responds by vocalizing in return. Piglets with greater needs than their littermates can communicate their heightened distress to the sow, who will show a much stronger response to their calls.

The piglets increasingly spend more time and venture greater distances away from the nest and with their mother abandon the nest where they were born after 7-14 days to join the rest of the group. The following weeks are a period of high social activity for the piglets as they interact with the other sows and their young.

The piglets begin to play, an important and natural activity, within the second week of life and engage in such group activities as chasing and frolicking, as well as individual play like rooting and using their mouths to examine novel objects. These activities continue into adulthood.

Within the sounder, if the other sows are also nursing litters, the mother pigs may share maternal duties, leaving each sow more time to forage alone. Adoption or nursing another sow's piglets, are not uncommon behaviors, and demonstrate a tendency towards communal dynamics.

At about eight weeks of age, the piglets are fully integrated in the group, although the social bonds among siblings remain strong. Weaning is a slow and gradual process, and the piglets continue to suckle until 14-17 weeks of age.

Pigs live in small, matriarchal groups, usually comprised of 2-6 sows and their young. Several sounders may form loose networks of related family groups, sharing overlapping home ranges.

Juvenile males stay with their family groups until the dominant males in the area force the younger males to leave at around 7-18 months of age, when the sows come into estrus. The juvenile males may then join a small bachelor group with other young adults before becoming more solitary as they age.

Kunekune Pig Society

Kunekune pigs were originally kept by Maoris in New Zealand. Their name is pronounced cooney cooney, which means fat and round in Maori. They did not originate in New Zealand, as it has no indigenous animals.

They are between twenty four and thirty inches high, and one hundred and twenty to two hundred and forty pounds in weight. They are completely covered in hair which can be anything between short and straight, and long and curly. They come in a range of cream, ginger, brown, black, and spotted. They have a medium to short snout, and either prick or flopped ears. They have short legs and a short round body. The most unusual feature of most Kunekune pigs is a pair of tassels (called piri piri) under their chin like a goat.

It is the smallest domesticated breed of pig in the world and is a favorite among pet pig owners, due to its friendly nature and love of human company.

Pigs Using Mirrors

A study of domesticated pigs found that with some experimenting they can find food based on a reflection in a mirror.

In the study, four pairs of domesticated pigs were allowed to familiarize themselves with a mirror for five hours. The study was conducted at Cambridge University in the U.K. and found that, given a chance to familiarize themselves with a mirror, many pigs can find food based only on its reflection in the mirror. The findings were published in the journal Animal Behavior.

After familiarization, each pig was placed in a pen with an angled mirror and a partition, behind which were treats such as apple slices or M&Ms. Seven of the eight pigs immediately looked behind the partition and found the food. A control group of pigs that had never seen a mirror before searched behind the mirror for the food.

A researcher said the study shows pigs have a high degree of assessment awareness, or the ability to use memories and observations to quickly learn to assess a situation and act on it.

Danes and Pigs

In Denmark, pigs outnumber people two to one. No traditional Danish meal would be complete without something wrapped in, around, or topped with pork.

In 2012, the country exported close to $6 billion in pig meat.

During 2013, a "pork quota" was given serious consideration at a national party meeting. The requirement was for menus at public institutions to contain at least twenty percent pig.

Mangalitsa Pigs

Big, fat, and curly haired Mangalicas, or Mangalitsas in English with paunchy bodies covered in tight curls like sheep. They have been nicknamed woolly pigs and curly haired hogs for their blonde, red, or black curls.

The Mangalitsa pig is a product of a 19th-century Austro-Hungarian experiment in cross breeding with a wild boar and a pig bred especially for lard.

The meat is a luscious red, more akin to beef than pork. It has a fifty percent fat content that gives it a coveted marble and buttery flavor. The breed nearly died out during the push for leaner and faster growing hogs, but in the early the 1990s it was revived by a Hungarian breeder. Today there are 60,000 purebred Mangalitsas worldwide, with about 50,000 in Hungary.

Charles Krausche raises his Mangalitsas at two farms in the Catskills US and sells to a few restaurants and specialty stores in the region. He is one of a small band of Mangalitsa farmers in the US.

Mangalitsas are more expensive to produce than other breeds, such as Berkshire and Ibérico pigs. They take about a year to grow to 300 to 350 pounds, versus six months for most commercial breeds. The pigs produce five to eight piglets per litter.

About half of the Mangalitsa is pure unprocessed fat. Lard is making a steady comeback and Mangalitsa lard is known for its flavor.

National Swine Resource and Research

The National Swine Resource and Research Center (NSRRC) was established in 2003 to develop the infrastructure to ensure that biomedical investigators across a variety of disciplines have access to critically needed swine models of human health and disease. The NSRRC also serves as a central resource for reagents, information, and training related to use of swine models in biomedical research.

Swine are the optimal model species for investigation of a large number of human diseases and have made valuable contributions to almost every field of human medicine. Swine share anatomic and physiologic characteristics with humans that make them ideal models for research. In addition, the anatomy and physiology make pig organs likely candidates for transplantation in humans.

National Swine Improvement Federation

Mission Statement: To advance and stimulate individual and collaborative efforts of swine breeding stock suppliers, academic personnel, and pork industry affiliates in the research, development, and utilization of scientifically-based genetic improvement programs and associated practices for the economically efficient production of high quality, nutritious pork.

National Pork Board

The National Pork Board will elevate U.S. pork as the global protein of choice by continuously and collaboratively working to do what's right for people, pigs and the planet. Mission: The National Pork Board is the catalyst that unites pork producers with key stakeholders focused on building a bright future for the pork industry through research, promotion and education.

Hog Offal and Scrapple

Offal, also called variety meats, or organ meats, refers to the internal organs and entrails of a butchered animal. The word does not refer to a particular list of edible organs, which vary by culture and region, but includes most internal organs excluding muscle and bone. As an English mass noun, the term offal has no plural form. Some cultures shy away from offal as food, while others use it as everyday food, or in delicacies.

Some offal dishes are considered gourmet food in international cuisine. This includes foie gras, pâté, and sweetbreads. Other offal dishes remain part of traditional regional cuisine and may be consumed especially in connection with holidays. This includes Scottish haggis, Jewish chopped liver, Southern US chitlins, Mexican menudo as well as many other dishes. Intestines are traditionally used as casing for sausages.

Swine Genomes

The Swine Genome Sequencing Consortium (SGSC) was formed in 2003 by academic, government, and industry representatives to provide international coordination for sequencing the pig genome. The SGSC's mission is to advance biomedical research for animal production and health by the development of DNA based tools and products resulting from the sequencing of the swine genome. During September, 2003, interested researchers convened at INRA Jouy-en-Josas to establish the SGSC for facilitation and coordination of international efforts toward obtaining the complete porcine genome sequence

The group web site does not seem to be very active during the past few years, with the exception of the above in a 2012 paper.

Pig DNA

Scientists announced that they have mapped the entire genome of the domestic pig, revealing that besides providing tasty bacon and sausages, the animal may also be useful in fighting human diseases.

The study published in the journal Nature found that pigs and humans share more than 100 DNA mutations that have previously been linked to diseases like obesity, diabetes, dyslexia, Parkinson's and Alzheimer's, according to US and European researchers.

"In total, we found 112 positions where the porcine protein has the same amino acid that is implicated in a disease in humans," researchers wrote.

Researchers said that because pigs share many of the same complex genetic diseases as humans, the animals would serve as excellent models for studying the underlying biology of human disease.

A domestic pig breed is already being used extensively in medical research because of its anatomical similarity to humans, and pig heart valves have been used by doctors to replace faulty human ones.

Scientists can use the new genome map to improve meat production by breeding a new generation of super-pigs that will grow faster, survive longer, produce more offspring and yield more meat for less feed.

"This new analysis helps us understand the genetic mechanisms that enable high-quality pork production, feed efficiency and resistance to disease," Sonny Ramaswany, director of the U.S. Department of

Agriculture's National Institute of Food and Agriculture said, according to Reuters.

Scientists in the sequencing project compared the domestic pig's genome to that of the wild boar, human, mouse, dog, horse, and cow.

A recent study also revealed that pigs had the most olfactory receptor genes, which highlights the importance of smell in the scavenger animal's lifestyle, and that pigs also had fewer bitter taste receptors meaning that "pigs can eat food that is unpalatable to humans," which is one of the reasons why pigs have become such a highly valued farm animal. *I am still trying to figure out how they will know if a pig has Alzheimer's.*

National Animal Genome Research

The US Pig Genome Project is supported by the USDA-NIFA National Animal Genome Research Program. NIFA-USDA is a member of the Animal Genomics Program Officers working group that has members from many and various federal agencies. This working group has explored common scientific areas of interest that are within the mission for the individual federal agencies.

Illumina and the International Porcine SNP Chip Consortium developed a porcine 60K+ SNP and has shipped it to many researchers worldwide. The bimonthly Pig Genome Update has published over 118 issues and has been distributed electronically to over 2,300 people worldwide.

Pig Islands

For some reason, many years ago man introduced pigs to tiny uninhabited **Clipperton Island**, about 800 miles off Acapulco Mexico. The pigs soon turned feral and began eating the eggs of the nesting Boobie sea birds. A few years ago, Ken Stager came to count the wildlife on Clipperton and brought with him a shotgun to shoot some birds for a museum. Instead, he saw what the pigs were doing to the birds and used his shotgun to kill all the pigs. True story.

Today Clipperton has 40,000 Masked Boobies and 20,000 Brown Boobies, among others, but no pigs and no men. Just goes to show you that if that island had been inhabited by man, who is naturally predisposed to bacon, then man, boobies, and pigs would have all lived in peace and harmony.

Pig Beach located on the uninhabited island of Big Major Cay, just North of Staniel Cay in the Exuma Cays of the Bahamas. The island is home to approximately twenty pigs and piglets, stray cats, and goats. Origins vary about how the pigs came there, but they get along with people well and can be seen swimming in the water, just off the beach.

Ossabaw Island Hogs

Early explorers brought livestock to the Americas beginning in the 1500s, including pigs that escaped or were deliberately set free in the New World. These pigs were the foundation for the historic populations of pigs in the southern United States. One of these is the Ossabaw, a free-range breed that is found on Ossabaw Island, off the coast of Georgia near Savannah. There is historic agreement that Ossabaw Island hogs have descended from foundation stock brought by Spanish explorers, inferring that the pigs are Spanish in origin. However, DNA analysis suggests that the Ossabaw Island pigs came from the Canary Islands, an important stop by the Spanish and Portuguese explorers en route to the New World. This reflects the influence of Asian pigs. The mtDNA of Spanish (or Iberian) pigs reflects only European influences. Additional genetic research is needed to understand the relationship of the pigs on the Canary Islands and on Ossabaw Island with Spanish pigs, including the paternal side of the DNA picture.

The Ossabaw pig breed is unusual and important for three reasons. Its history as an isolated island population has meant that the Ossabaw is the closest genetic representative of historic stocks brought over by the Spanish. Second, the presence of pigs on Ossabaw Island provides scientists with an exceptional opportunity to study a long-term natural population. Third, the Ossabaw breed is biologically unique, having been shaped by natural selection in a challenging environment known for heat, humidity, and seasonal scarcity of food. Ossabaw hogs may be as small as 100 pounds, but they are able to store astounding amounts of body fat in order to survive during the seasons when there is little to eat. This biochemical adaptation is similar to non-insulin dependent diabetes in humans, making the pigs a natural animal model for this disease. The pigs are also highly tolerant of dietary salt. Ossabaw Island hogs on the mainland, once removed from the selective pressures of their island home, have lost some of their unique survival adaptations.

Ossabaw hogs are usually black, although some are black with white spots or light with black spots. Adult pigs are very hairy with heavy bristles on the head, neck and topline. The frayed tips of the bristles, a primitive characteristic, are another indication of the distinctiveness of the population. Their snouts are long and slightly dished. Heads and shoulders of the hogs are heavy, and while they seem out of proportion to the rest of the body, that impression belies the speed and agility of these animals in the dense undergrowth of the island.

Boston Butt

This cut of meat does not mean "butt" as in "rear end" - the cut actually comes from the front shoulder of the pig.

During colonial days New England butchers tended to take less prized cuts of pork like these and pack them into barrels for storage and transport. The barrels the pork went into were called butts. (A hogshead is 64.8 US gallons and butt is equal to two US hogsheads or 126 US gallons.)

This particular shoulder cut became known around the country as a New England specialty, and hence it became the "Boston butt." *Interesting that this name is not used in Boston.*

Cultured Pork

Sounds like an oxymoron doesn't it. Scientists from Eindhoven University in The Netherlands have for the first time grown pork meat in the laboratory by extracting cells from a live pig and growing them in a petri dish.

The scientists, led by Professor of Physiology Mark Post, extracted myoblast cells from a living pig and grew them in a solution of nutrients derived from the blood of animal fetuses (although they intend to replace the solution with a synthesized alternative in the future).

As long as the final product looks and tastes like meat, Post said he is convinced people will buy it.

At present the product is a sticky, soggy, and unappetizing muscle mass, but the team is seeking ways to exercise and stretch the muscles to turn the product into meat of a more familiar consistency. Post described the current in-vitro meat product as resembling wasted muscle, but he is confident they can improve its texture. Nobody has yet tasted the cultured meat because laboratory rules prevent the scientists tasting the product themselves.

The research is partly funded by the Dutch government, but is also backed by the Dutch sausage-making firm Stegeman, owned by Sara Lee.

The scientists believe the meat product may be available for use in sausages within five years.

Other groups are also working on trying to produce cultured meat. NASA has funded research in the US on growing fish chunks from cells and meat from turkey cells, with the idea that the technology could have wide application in future space travel, since growing edible muscle would allow future astronauts to avoid a range of problems associated with using live animals in space.

The reaction of vegetarian groups has been mixed. A representative of PETA (People for the Ethical Treatment of Animals) said as long as the meat was not the flesh of a dead animal there would be no ethical objection. Last year PETA even offered a prize of $1 million to the first person or group who could come up with a commercially viable cultured meat product.

RSPCA

Taken from the RSPCA Australia knowledgebase - 'Free range', 'bred free range', 'organic' and 'sow-stall free' are terms that are applied to animal-based food products, such as meat or eggs. They refer to the systems used for housing farm animals. Unfortunately, there are no universally accepted definitions for these terms.

Free-range pork

Free-range pork comes from pigs that were born and raised with free access to the outdoors. That is, where the sows and growing piglets have access to paddocks, as well as huts or other forms of housing for shelter, and are not confined to sow stalls (for pregnant sows) or farrowing crates (for lactating sows and their piglets).

Bred free-range pork

'Bred free range' is a term used to apply to pig products (pork, bacon, etc) from pigs that were born in a free-range environment, but were subsequently raised indoors. These pigs may be raised in large open sheds with straw bedding or in small pens on concrete floors as in conventional pig farming systems.

Sow-stall free pork

The Australian pig industry has committed to phasing out sow stalls and moving all female breeding pigs (sows) to indoor group housing. The term 'sow-stall free' is used to differentiate pork product from pigs that have been born to sows in group housing. The pig industry defines 'sow-stall free' as a system where a sow may have been kept in a stall for up to 5 days following last mating up to one week before farrowing; however, other definitions allow only one day in a stall. These stalls are called 'mating stalls', are very similar to a sow stall, and are used at mating to prevent aggression between sows and hence potential injury or abortion. Following this period of confinement, the sow is housed in groups with other pregnant sows.

The move from sow stalls to group housing is a very important first step. The next priority is transitioning away from farrowing crates which may be used to confine the sow for up to five weeks (from about a week before giving birth to her piglets up until they are weaned). Farrowing pens which allow the sow freedom of movement while protecting the piglets from crushing are under development. Piglets from sow-stall free sows may be raised in large open sheds with straw bedding or in small pens on concrete floors as in conventional pig farming systems.

Pigs and Xenografts

The US Department of Health and Human Services data shows the total waiting list of candidates is 122,407 people needing a lifesaving organ transplant.

The total number of donors from January through May 2015 was 5,975. On average, 22 people die each day while waiting for a transplant. Every 10 minutes someone is added to the national transplant waiting list.

Xenotransplantation research is being carried out by a regenerative-medicine division of a biotech company, Revivicor and the company is United Therapeutics.

Their work is producing genetically engineered pigs to provide human-compatible cells for organs and tissues to be used in transplant surgery, or xenografts. The pigs are "humanized" with the addition of as many as five human genes to stop organ rejection. The genetic changes also make the organs more compatible with a human body.

The researchers say they have kept a pig heart alive in a baboon for 945 days. They also reported the longest-ever kidney swap between these species, lasting 136 days.

Hog Numbers

As of December, 2014 The total US hog population was 66.05 million. Pork production will climb during 2015 to a record 23.908 billion pounds. About 547,800 U.S. jobs are involved in various aspects of the pork industry. Overall, an estimated $22.3 billion of personal income and $39 billion of gross national product are supported by the hog industry.

Total sales from the pork production and processing sectors support additional input purchases, spending on transportation and other services, as well as consumer-related purchases worth nearly $122 billion of direct and indirect sales throughout the U.S. economy. During 2014, the US exported 2,178,484 metric tons of pork around the world.

Cost of Bacon

Pork bellies, the raw material for bacon, once contributed greatly to summer-demand strength with the popularity of BLTs. However, increased year-round use of bacon by foodservice operations has removed much of the seasonal variation in bacon use and belly prices.

Holiday ham demand causes ham prices to vary counter-seasonally to hog prices, with the year's lowest ham prices in the summer and the highest prices usually in October and November.

Did You Know

Many places around the world refer to 'hair of the dog' to mean a hangover recipe, but in Costa Rica the same expression is used, but it refers to a pig as in: **hair of the same pig**.

Oxford University Press Guidelines - The news is Oxford University Press has issued guidelines instructing authors of children's books to avoid references to pigs, sausage, or anything else that might be construed as porcine for fear of offending Muslims. It has no specific policies issued instructing authors not to offend Christians.

July 17 is **Yellow Pig Day**, a Princeton mathematician's holiday celebrating yellow pigs and the number 17. It is celebrated annually since the early 1960's, primarily on college campuses, and primarily by mathematicians. On campus, Yellow Pig Cake and Yellow Pig Carols are tradition!

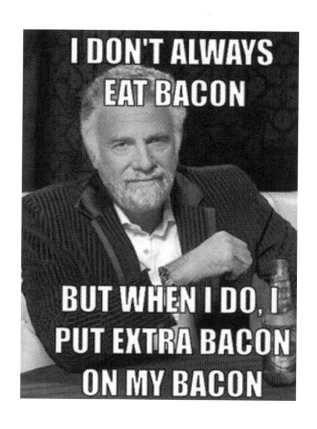

Bacon is the pithy part of pork

BACON FACTS

Below, for your enlightenment and reading pleasure is a compendious oddments of all things bacon.

- In England, a slice of bacon is known as a rasher. In the US it can mean more than one slice.

- Seventy percent of the bacon in America is consumed at the breakfast table.

- The USDA defines "bacon" as "the cured belly of a swine carcass." *Sounds like Homer Simpson, "Ah sweet savory swine carcass..."*

- A 200 pound pig will yield close to 20 pounds of bacon, along with other popular meat products.

- Bacon may be eaten smoked, boiled, broiled, fried, baked, grilled, or used as a major or minor ingredient to flavor other dishes. Bacon is also used for barding (attaching strips of bacon) and larding roasts, especially game, such as venison or pheasant.

- In Europe, this part of the pig is usually not smoked like bacon is in the United States. It is used primarily in cubes (lardons) as a cooking ingredient and is valued both as a source of fat and for its flavor. In Italy, this is called pancetta and is usually cooked in small cubes or served uncooked and thinly sliced as part of an antipasto.

- Historically, "ham" and "bacon" referred to different cuts of meat that were brined or packed identically, often together in the same barrel.

- Americans consume an average of 18 pounds of bacon per year.

- Bacon sales in US for the year 2013 were $3.7 billion.

- Currently more than half of US households have bacon available and more than half of US restaurants have bacon on the menu. In 2012, twenty percent of the respondents stated they had eaten one pound of bacon within the last 30 days.

- Fifty Nine percent of bacon is consumed during the week and forty nine percent on the weekend.

- Bacon is one of the oldest processed meats in history.

- Bacon makes us feel happy, satisfied, blissful, which greatly reduces stress and effectively relieves the negative effects of frustration and self deprivation.

- Bacon provides us with substantial amounts of the important, necessary vitamins and minerals our bodies need to function healthfully. From bacon, we receive: 65% of the Recommended Daily Intake of Thiamin (Vitamin B1) as well as 47% of Niacin (Vitamin B3), 38% of Vitamin B12, 36% of Zinc, 24% of Vitamin B6, 22% of Riboflavin (Vitamin B2), 22% of Phosphorus, 10% of Pantothenate, 10% of Magnesium, 9% of Iron. The Protein to fat balance in bacon is 4 to 1, which is one of the highest protein to fat balances found in any meat, fish, or fowl found on Earth.

- The formula for bacon cologne was invented in 1920 by French butcher John Fargginay.

- Raising pigs for food dates back to 7000 B.C. in the Middle East. Some historians say that bacon made from immature hogs was a favorite of the early Romans and Greeks.

- About 500 years ago, bacon or bacoun referred to all pork.

- Seventy percent of bacon in the US is eaten at breakfast.

- Pork bellies have been traded on the Chicago Mercantile Exchange since 1961. The unit of trading is 20 tons of frozen, trimmed bellies.

- People in the US consume 32 billion slices of bacon per year.

- Bacon Day is held on the Saturday before Labor Day.

- The most popular flavors of bacon are hickory, maple, applewood, mesquite, honey, sugared, peppered.

- Bacon explosion has become one of the most popular meals in the world. It is made with a bacon weave wrapped around a filling of spiced sausage and crumbled bacon.

- WebMD reports that two pork sausage links contain 140 calories and 12 grams of fat. Three strips of pan-fried hickory smoked bacon contain 120 calories and 9 grams of fat.

- Baconnaise (Bacon flavored mayonnaise) is actually vegetarian (as are most store bacon bits).

- Bacon contains six types of Umami, which produces an addictive neurochemical response.

- Each year in the US, more than 2 billion pounds of bacon are sold according to the National Pork Board.

- There are varieties of beer, vodka, and bourbon flavored with bacon.

- The British spend around £1.37billion a year on bacon, eating 227,000 tonnes of it.

- The word "bacon" dates back to the late 1500s.

- Four sizzling strips of pan-fried bacon have 168 calories. Two large scrambled eggs have 182 calories.

- More than ten bacon sandwiches are eaten every second on average in the UK.

- According to a recent survey, 46 per cent of people like to grill bacon while 37 per cent fry it.

- When Julius Caesar landed in Britain in 55BC, he brought his own bacon with him.

- The earliest known reference to 'streaky bacon' is in Charles Dickens' Oliver Twist.

- George Orwell wrote of a 'bacon sandwich' in 1931, but the first mention of a 'bacon sarnie' in print was in the Daily Express on August 21, 1986.

- BLT became popular after WWII when lettuce and tomatoes became available in stores all year.

- Oscar Mayer patented packaged sliced bacon in 1924.

- In the US, bacon is eaten 70% breakfast, 11% lunch, 17% dinner, and 2% snack.

- A rasher of bacon as found on restaurant menus means a serving, typically more than one slice.

- Bacon is prepared from several different cuts of meat. It is usually made from side and back cuts of pork, except in the United States, where it is almost always prepared from pork belly. The side cut has more meat and less fat than the belly. Bacon may be prepared from either of two distinct back cuts: fatback, which is almost pure fat, and pork loin, which is very lean.

- Bacon is Gluten Free.

- Almost half of bacon fat is monounsaturated, just like olive oil. It can actually lower bad cholesterol.

- The restaurant chain first to put bacon on a cheeseburger was A&W.

- Bacon cost sixteen cents a pound in 1912.

- A side of unsliced bacon was once known as a flitch, but now is known as a slab.

- Uncured Bacon is in fact, still cured. However, the difference is in the curing process. Natural nitrates found in celery powder or juice and sea salt are used in uncured bacon to obtain a similar taste without using sodium nitrates. Whether cured or uncured, both generally have the same nutrition, including calories and fat, but some uncured bacon may be higher in sodium to replace the lost sodium nitrates.

- An individual slice of bacon is a slice or strip.

- The difference between bacon and salted pork or ham is primarily in the brine used. Brine for bacon often includes sodium nitrite, sodium nitrate, and saltpeter for curing the meat; sodium ascorbate for setting the color, as well as speeding up the curing process; and brown or maple sugar for flavor, among other ingredients. One of the principle differences is that brine for ham tends to have a much higher concentration of sugar.

- 90.4% of Brits have bacon in their homes.

- A typical American eats 28 pigs in his/her lifetime.

- Bacon actually is good for the brains of unborn children. Bacon contains a nutrient called choline which has been shown to boost the intelligence of people. You can also get choline from eggs, liver, milk, chicken, and various nuts.

- There are about 150 volatile organic compounds that contribute to bacon's meaty aroma, many of them hydrocarbons and aldehydes, with some nitrogen-containing compounds thrown in for good measure.

- There are four basic components to bacon's overall taste. These are saltiness, smokiness, sweetness and leanness. Together these constitute balanced bacon.

- The earliest Christians, who lived in Israel, like the Jews did not eat pork, but by about 50 AD many Christians came from places where people did eat pork and the Christians decided that this rule did not apply to them.

- The first recorded spelling of the family name is shown to be that of William Bacun, circa 1150, in the "Chartulary of Staffordshire", during the reign of King Stephen, known as "The Count of Blois", 1135 - 1154.

Crest for the Bacon Family

It is typically red and has variations, as do many family crests.

Bacon Butty

Bacon butty is Britain's number one snack. More than half the nation reaches for it according to a poll of 2,000 adults.

A bacon sandwich, known in parts of the United Kingdom and New Zealand as a bacon butty or bacon sarnie, in Ireland as a rasher sandwich, and as a bacon sanger in Australia. In parts of Scotland is a sandwich of cooked bacon between bread that is usually spread with butter or margarine.

Breakfast is the most popular time to eat bacon sandwiches, while almost 40 per cent of those polled admitted also liking them for lunch.

Prime minister, David Cameron is a fan of bacon butties. Daniel Craig, (James Bond), demands them on the set when he is filming and has them flown in from England.

According to a scientific study (True), an integral part of a successful bacon butty is the aural factor - how loud the crunch is when you bite into it. A classic bacon butty is soft white bread, butter, bacon fat, crispy bacon.

UK Bacon Study

Bacon topped a list of Britain's favorite 100 foods. Britain's first ever Top 100 Food Index is a comprehensive study into what now makes up favorite tastes. The research was commissioned by Food Network UK.

One in ten Brits named the breakfast and sandwich favorite their top food, followed by chicken, chocolate, and steak.

The study indicates 67 per cent of Brits saying their favorite food has also been the same for the past ten years, and a third claim they could eat their favorite food every day without ever tiring of it.

Nitrates and Nitrites

Now Non-Issues: The fact is, while it is true that nitrates and nitrites are unhealthy for your body, what most pro-veggie, chicken, and fish nutritionists fail to tell you is that you can easily avoid nitrates and nitrites by simply not burning / charring / over cooking your bacon, or by baking your bacon in the oven.

Some people also choose to avoid nitrates and nitrites by cooking their bacon in the microwave, however, some medical research shows a strong correlation between micro-waved proteins (all meats and proteins, from beef to fish, from cheese to eggs, and even milk) and cancers caused by protein mutation under the conditions of microwave bombardment. *I recommend using the oven, 400 degrees, 8 to 10 minutes per side.*

If you always include some dairy and citrus in your bacon meal, the vitamins A, D and E work to effectively prevent conversion of nitrates and nitrites into "nitrosamines" in the stomach, rendering them harmless to the body.

Bacon Shortage

It has become more expensive than in the past, because of shortage of supply and increased demand. On the store shelves, average retail prices rose more than $1 per pound since 2011, to more than $4, according to US Department of Agriculture. This is happening in the middle of other price reductions and discounts, due to the poor economy.

Bacon was once thought of only a breakfast food, but now is a round-the-clock food showing up as a garnish on many dishes, including chocolate items. One analyst suggests that demand is up because restaurants, seeking to regain business lost to the tight economy, have been adding more bacon to sandwiches and salads to spice up flavors. . . and bills.

Bacon Laser

A team of Harvard scientists has paved the way for a deadly laser pig weapon by demonstrating that, with a little encouragement, pig fat cells can be made to lase. According to *MIT Technology Review*, Seok Hyun Yun and Matjaž Humar stimulated spheres of fat inside porcine cells with an optical fiber, causing them to emit laser light. Pig cells contain "nearly perfectly spherical" fat balls, which are conducive to lasing by resonance when supplied with a suitable light source.

Seok Hyun Yun, lead author of the report which appears in *Nature Photonics*, thinks an ultimate use of his work might be to deploy "intracellular micro lasers as research tools, sensors, or perhaps as part of a drug treatment". Russ Algar of the University of British Columbia classified the ground-breaking research as of little practical use, but admitted it was "very cool."

Canadians Love Bacon

In a survey by Maple Leaf Foods:

* 43% of the respondents said they would rather have bacon than sex
* 23% of men ranked bacon as their number one favorite fragrance
* 82% said they love bacon and also said they are good lovers
* 23% wondered if 'my partner loves bacon more than me'

The survey was conducted among 1,006 randomly selected Canadian adults. The results of the online survey have been statistically weighted according to the most current education, age, gender and region census data to ensure samples representative of the entire adult population of Canada. *No word yet on whether the Addy family was included in the survey.*

Bring Home the Bacon

The current definition means to earn money, especially for one's family.

Great Britain shares a love of all things porcine and especially bacon. Some of the information below comes from the English Breakfast Society

"Bring home the bacon" is based on the story of a local couple who, in 1104, impressed the Prior of Little Dunmow (Essex, England) with their marital devotion to the point that he award them a flitch (side) of bacon. A husband who could bring home the bacon was held in high esteem by the community for his forbearance. The town still has 'Dunmow Flitch Trials' every 4 years and awards a flitch (a salted and cured side) of bacon to married couples if they can satisfy the judge and jury of 6 maidens and 6 bachelors that in twelve months and a day they have not wished themselves unmarried again.

Another source for this comes from the old sport of catching a greased pig at country fairs. The winner kept the pig and brought home the bacon.

The continuing ritual of couples showing their devotion and winning the prize, to considerable acclimation by the local populace, is old and well authenticated. Geoffrey Chaucer mentions it in The Wife of Bath's Tale and Prologue, from 1395: "But never for us the flitch of bacon though, That some may win in Essex at Dunmow."

The derivation of the phrase is also muddled by association with other bacon expressions, as save one's bacon, etc. In reality, the link between them is limited to the fact that bacon has been a slang term for one's body, and by extension one's livelihood or income, since the 17th century.

Living High on the Hog

The saying may have originated among army enlisted men, who received shoulder and leg cuts while their officers received choice cuts from the loin.

Pig in a Poke

It is an offering or deal that is foolishly accepted without being examined first. 'Don't buy a pig in a poke' might seem odd and archaic language. It's true that the phrase is very old, but actually it can be taken literally and remains good advice.

The advice being given is, don't buy a pig until you have seen it. In British commercial law it is 'caveat emptor' - Latin for 'let the buyer beware'. This remains the guiding principle of commerce in many countries and supports the view that if you buy something you take responsibility to ensure it is what you intended to buy.

A poke is a sack or bag. It has a French origin as 'poque' and, like several other French words, it's a diminutive formed by adding 'ette' or 'et' - hence 'pocket' really means 'small bag'. Poke is still in use in several English-speaking countries, notably Scotland and southeastern USA, and describes a type of bag that would be useful for carrying a piglet to market.

A pig that's in a poke might not be a pig. If a merchant tried to cheat by substituting a lower value animal, the trick could be uncovered by letting the 'cat out of the bag'. People have been repeating it for at least five hundred years.

Piggyback

Back in the 16th century, goods were transported in packs that people carried on theirs or animals backs. The term used to describe this was "pick pack" because you would pick up a pack in order to carry it on your back.

"Pick pack" eventually became "pick-a-pack" as in pick a pack and carry it on your back. Eventually, because an individual was picking a pack to carry on his back, the term "pick-a-pack" became "pick-a-back".

Turns out, though, that the insertion of the "a" caused a problem and ultimately paved the way for the original phrase "pick pack" to become "piggyback". Due to the pronunciation of the term as a whole, "pick-a-pack" often sounded like "pick -i-back" which sounded like "picky back". This ultimately gave rise to the term "piggyback" around this time for people carrying a pack on their back and by the 1930s, the definition further progressed to describe riding on someone's back and shoulders. The pig was the only animal that sounded like "picky" and "pickyback" became piggyback.

Blind Pig

The terms 'blind pig' and 'blind tiger' originated in the United States during the 19th century. These terms were applied to lower-class establishments that sold alcoholic beverages illegally, and the terms are still in use today. The operator of a saloon or bar would charge customers to see an attraction, such as an animal and then serve a complimentary alcoholic beverage, thus circumventing the law. These words came before US Prohibition (1920 - 1933).

A speakeasy, also called a blind pig is an establishment that illegally sells alcoholic beverages. The phrase 'speak easy shop', denoting a place where unlicensed liquor sales were made, appeared in a British naval memoir written in 1844. The phrase, 'speak softly shop', meaning a "smuggler's house," appeared in a British slang dictionary published in 1823.

Piggy Banks

Many years ago, dishes and cookware in Europe were made of a dense, orange clay called pygg. When people saved coins in jars made of this clay, the jars became known as 'pygg banks'. Over the next few hundred years, as the English language evolved, the clay (pygg) and the animal (pigge) came to be pronounced the same, and people slowly forgot that pygg once referred to the earthenware pots. During the 19th century when English potters received requests for pygg banks, they started producing banks shaped like pigs.

Australian Bacon Labels

New 'Made in Australia' labels are due to start in 2016 and feature the green and gold kangaroo triangle with added extras. It shows whether food products have been grown in Australia, and produced from 100 per cent, 75 per cent, 50 per cent, or less of Australian ingredients. The Government says this reformed Australian-made label is about Australians consumers supporting local farmers and the pork industry is delighted. The new system does not allow imported pork products made into bacon or ham, with a Made in Australia claim on its own.

Bacon wraps are like giving hugs to your food.

TYPES OF PIG BACON

American Bacon, Side Bacon, or Streaky Bacon

- as the British call it, is generally cut from the belly of the pig, which is not actually its stomach but the fat-streaked padding on the side of the animal. It is very fatty with long layers of fat running parallel to the rind.

Back Bacon, Irish Bacon, or Canadian Bacon

- because it comes from the loin in the middle of the back of the pig. If Canadian bacon is cured, it is usually done in a basic brine. Sometimes it is smoked, but not always. Canadian back bacon is a very lean, meaty cut of bacon, with less fat compared to other cuts. *Someone once referred to back bacon as, 'Slab of pig consumed by Canadians and served fried with Kraft Dinner, beer, and cigarettes'.*

British Bacon

- comes from a combination of pork loin and pork belly. It leaves much fat on the loin, especially the fat cap, and includes the part where the loin attaches to the same cut American-style is made from, the belly.

Collar Bacon

- is taken from the back of a pig near the head.

Cottage Bacon

- is thinly sliced lean pork from a shoulder cut that is typically oval shaped and meaty. It is cured and then sliced into round pieces for baking or frying.

Green Bacon

- is cold smoked. It is first cured using large amount of salt, either in brine or in dry packing. The result is fresh bacon or green bacon, which may then be further dried for weeks or months in cold air, boiled, or smoked. Fresh and dried bacon is typically cooked before eating. Boiled bacon and some smoked bacon can be eaten as is or may be cooked further before eating.

Jowl Bacon or Guanciale

- is an Italian specialty bacon, cured and smoked cheeks of pork, made by drying the meat from a hog's jowls. Its leaner than traditional pork pieces and has a richer flavor. It has three-week drying period.

Hock Bacon

- comes from the hog ankle joint between the ham and the foot. It is cured differently than ham hock.

Lardons or Lardoons

- are the part of the pig American bacon is made from. It is typically sliced into cubes. This is popular in continental Europe and used as a cooking ingredient due to its high fat and rich flavor. Lardons are not normally smoked, and are made from pork that has been cured with salt.

Middle Bacon

- from the side of the animal, is intermediate in cost, fat content, and flavor between streaky bacon and back bacon.

Pancetta

- is Italian streaky bacon, usually unsmoked, with a strong flavor. It is generally rolled up into cylinders after curing. In America unsmoked streaky bacon is often referred to as side pork.

Picnic or Café Bacon

- is from the picnic cut, which includes the shoulder beneath the blade. It is fairly lean, but tougher than most pork cuts. It comes from various off cuts of pork that are pressed into a pseudo-bacon shape. This is one of the least desirable types of bacon.

Slab Bacon

- typically has a medium to very high amount of fat. It is made from the belly and side cuts, and can come from fatback. Slab bacon is not to be confused with salt pork, which is prepared from the same cuts, but is not cured.

Speck or Kaiserfleisch

- is made by German and Austrian butchers and is made like pancetta.

Wild Boar Bacon

- is processed the same as pork bellies. Wild boar fat is much more potent that domestic pig and has a less or more sweet flavor, depending on the boar's diet. It tends to be more meaty and less fat. Some cannot tell the difference.

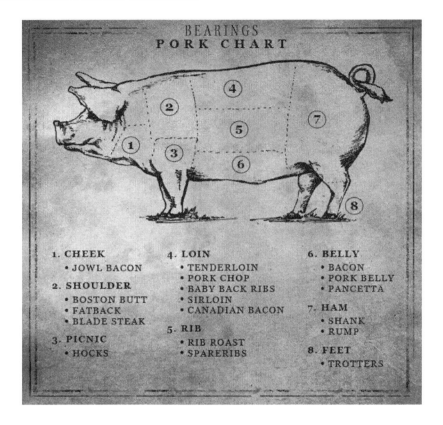

How Bacon is Made

YouTube has a great overview of how bacon is made:

http://www.youtube.com/watch?feature=player_embedded&v=_tvx_CKB7uI

Bacon is caviar of the gods.

TYPES OF NON PIG BACON

Not sure if I should have included this blasphemy, but to be fair minded to the infidels, here it is. It is well known fact that bacon has returned more vegans to the meat eating fold than any other food. A few of these items are for those who are still seeking direction and will try anything, like dieters who eat low fat Oreos. *I understand some folks actually believe these substitutes are tolerable to eat.*

Beef Bacon

Beef bacon is usually smokier, browner, leaner, and more chewy than crisp. Cured beef bacon tends to be a bit dry and lackluster compared to pork bacon.

Duck Bacon

It is widely and can be found in most major grocery stores. It does not taste like bacon. It is cut to look like bacon, although it just looks like dark duck meat cut in strips, not marbled bacon. You would not mistake the taste for pork, but it does have some of the familiar salty, sweet, smoky endorphin triggers that real bacon does.

Recipe - 4 cups cold water, 1 cup kosher salt, 2 1/2 tablespoons curing salt, 3/4 cup brown sugar, 3/4 cup brewed strong coffee, 3/4 cup pure maple syrup, 3 cups ice, 6 duck breast halves or 3 whole breasts

In a large bowl, dissolve kosher and curing salts in the cold water. Stir in brown sugar and mix until mostly dissolved, then add coffee and maple syrup. Finally add ice to the brine to keep the liquid cold and slow salt absorption. Add the brine to the container or bag holding the duck breasts. Cover tightly and place in refrigerator for 8 hours, then remove the breasts, rinse and dry overnight or let dry for 3-4 hours before smoking). Once completely dry, cold smoke according to your preferred method.

Lamb Bacon

Lamb bacon is usually made from the usually discarded lamb flap or lamb belly and is a lot thinner than its pork counterpart. It is cured to give it a bacon taste, but has a lamb flavor and smokiness and much fattier than pork bacon.

Recipe - Pour two cups of salt and one cup of sugar into a shallow baking pan. Coat the lamb on all sides, shake off the excess and wrap tightly in plastic wrap to ensure that the salt and sugar remain in constant contact with the meat. Refrigerate for two to four days until the meat is firm to the touch. Roast or smoke for 2 1/2 hours at 250 degrees, or until the internal temperature reaches 140 degrees.

Macon

This is another alternative to bacon, produced by curing cuts of mutton in a manner similar to the production of pork bacon. (Mutton is meat from a sheep that is older than a year, ideally 3 years of age.) Historically produced in Scotland, it was introduced across Britain during World War II as a consequence of rationing. It is today available as an alternative to bacon, produced for the Muslim market and sold at Halal butchers; it is largely similar in appearance to pork bacon except for the color, which tends to be black and yellow.

Schmacon

Howard Bender created Schmacon, which is bacon made from beef. He spent three years and hundreds of thousands of dollars developing Schmacon. It is not kosher. Schmacon and schmacon bits have lower fat, sodium and calories than traditional bacon. The product tastes kind of like pork bacon, kind of like pastrami, with a smoky maple finish. Schmacon won a 2014 food and beverage innovation award from the National Restaurant Association. Bender says, "Turkey bacon sucks."

Shitake Bacon

Vegans attempt to make bacon out of anything. Eggplant, coconut, mushrooms and tempeh have all been used to recreate various crispy and salty bacon analogs. It shows that the smoky savory quality of bacon might be imitated (but not duplicated) using completely vegan ingredients.

1 Tb olive oil
1/4 tsp salt
3/4 tsp liquid smoke
1 tsp sesame oil
1/2 tsp smoked paprika (optional)
2 cups shiitake mushroom caps, sliced thinly
Preheat oven to 350.

Combine all of the ingredients except for the sliced shiitake into a shallow bowl. Add in the sliced shiitake, and stir gently to combine. Allow to marinate at least an hour. Place the shiitake in a single layer onto a baking pan. Bake for 10 minutes, flip and bake for an additional 15 minutes. Increase the heat to 375 and bake for 10 minutes more.

Flip, then finish for 10 more minutes. Remove from the oven and place on paper towels to drain and serve while warm.

Tofu Bacon

1 package of firm tofu
1 Tb liquid smoke
sea salt
tamari or soy sauce
vegetable oil

Slice tofu on long side into 1/8th to 1/4th inch slices. In skillet add enough oil to just cover bottom and place slices in pan. Sprinkle with sea salt and liquid smoke. Sauté over low to med. heat until golden brown, flip and brown on other side, about 20 minutes. After golden brown, sprinkle soy sauce over slices and sauté another 4 to 5 minutes.

Turkey Bacon

Turkey bacon and vegetarian bacon, also referred to as fakon, veggie bacon, or vacon, is a turkey product marketed as a bacon alternative, and available in supermarkets. It is high in protein and fiber, low in fat, and has no cholesterol. Two slices average 75 calories. Vegetarian bacon is also easy to make at home by marinating strips of tempeh or tofu in various spices and then deep frying. *People who think turkey or vegan bacon bears any relationship to real bacon should be boiled in brine and hung out to dry.*

Vegan Bacon

Coconut Bacon can replicate a baconish flavor and crispness with coconut flakes. Maybe it is one step closer to get them to real bacon, of which there is no substitute.

2 tablespoons tamari or soy sauce
1 tablespoon liquid smoke
1 tablespoon pure maple syrup
1/2 teaspoon smoked paprika
3 1/2 cups large flaked coconut (about a 7 oz.)
mineral salt for sprinkling,
coconut oil, for greasing
Preheat oven to 325 degrees.

Mix the first four ingredients in a small bowl making sure to break up any clumps of paprika. In a large bowl add coconut flakes, drizzle the wet mixture over top and toss making sure to coat each flake well.

Using a slotted spoon, scoop seasoned coconut flakes and place onto a lightly greased, or parchment paper lined, cookie sheets in a single layer as much as possible. Sprinkle coconut flakes lightly with a bit of salt if desired.

Place in oven and bake for 20-25 minutes. Set the timer for intervals of 5 minutes and stir each time making sure to rearrange all pieces by bringing the center to the outside and the outside to the center for even cooking. After the first 15 minutes, watch closely as it can burn very quickly. Remove when coconut has a browned and caramelized color. Let cool, it will get crispy as it cools. Once completely cooled you can store leftovers in an air tight container and keep in the pantry for up to a week or two. If it softens a bit, re-crisp under broiler for a few minutes. For a more intense smoke flavor, add up to 1 tablespoon more of the liquid smoke of choice.

Vegan Bacon Grease - Mix coconut oil, non-gmo soy protein, sea salt, pure maple syrup, black pepper, onion, garlic, torula yeast, natural smoke flavor.

Vegetarian Bacon

This is also referred to as fakon, veggie bacon, or vacon, and available in supermarkets. It has no cholesterol, is low in fat, and contains large amounts of protein and fiber. Two slices contain about 74 calories. Vegetarian bacon is usually made from marinated strips of tempeh.

Dulse

Scientists have developed a new strain of dulse, a marine algae seaweed with twice the nutritional profile of kale and a strong bacon flavor. It is currently harvested and usually sold for up to $90 a pound in dried form as a cooking ingredient or nutritional supplement. The newly developed strain resembles translucent red lettuce and is full of antioxidants, minerals, protein, and vitamins. When fried, it tastes like bacon, not seaweed. *Not sure I am ready to trust the taste buds of scientists, especially for bacon taste.*

A baconista is one who both prepares and serves bacon.

PORCINEOGRAPH MAP OF UNITED STATES

The Porcineograph, produced by the Forbes Lithographic Manufacturing Company of Boston around 1876 defines the states and territories of the US in terms of their regional foods. Even back then pork products and bacon dominated.

- Arizona: Jerked Beef and Greasy Doings;
  California: Bear Steaks, Grapes and Ham Sandwich;
  Connecticut: Shad, Hog's Head Cheese and Gingerbread;
  Florida: Turtle Soup, Oranges and Pickled Trotters;
  Kansas: Buffalo Tongues, Paw-Paw and Ham;
  Maine: Lobsters, Cunners, Pork-Apple-Pie and Baked Indian;
  Louisiana:P Gumbo Soup, Poussoneau and Larded Beef;
  Minnesota: Gopher, Stewed Pork and Molasses;
  Mississippi: Persimmon, Bacon and Hoe Cake;
  New Jersey, Pork Pie, Peaches and Pigeons;
  New York, Roast Pig, Fried Oysters, Strawberry Shortcake & Uninvestigated Drinks;
  Ohio: Sugar-cured Ham, Cream Cheese and Catawba Grapes;
  Tennessee: "Uncle Ned", Bacon Roasting Ears and Corn Cake;
  Texas: Wild Steer and Corn Dodgers wobbled in Pork Fat;
  Vermont: Hasty Pudding, Maple Syrup, Succotash and Pork;
  Wisconsin: Boiled Hog's Heads, Hulled Barley and Blood Pudding.

[Map source: the Library of Congress.]

*Too much of anything is bad, but
too much bacon is hardly enough.*

NEW FOOD PYRAMIDS

Bacon, the foundation for all diets.

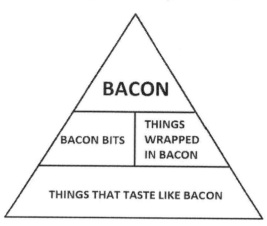

BACON

BACON BITS | THINGS WRAPPED IN BACON

THINGS THAT TASTE LIKE BACON

Fats, oils & sweets

Milk

Meat, meat substitutes & other proteins

Vegetables

Fruits

BACON!!

TOP REASONS WHY BACON IS HEALTHY

- Several slices of bacon are healthier in terms of calories, salt, fat and cholesterol than a hot dog, hamburger, or glazed donut.

- The protein found in bacon is extremely valuable to maintaining our energy level and a fully functioning, healthy body, with a minimum of fat building carbohydrates.

- Traditional pork bacon is high in protein, vitamins and minerals, including B6, B12, niacin, thiamin, riboflavin, iron, magnesium, potassium and zinc, as well as choline, a nutrient which helps improve cognitive performance, memory, mood, and mental alertness.

- Several university and medical center studies have shown that including bacon as a regular, part of your diet naturally works to lower the body's blood pressure and blood sugar levels, helping to prevent or alleviate the effects of diabetes, as well as heart disease, stroke, and heart attack.

- Bacon helps to fully satiate your appetite with high protein, low carb energy, helping the body lose weight, raise metabolism and build leaner, stronger muscles.

- Bacon has less total fat, saturated fat and cholesterol than many popular cuts of beef and chicken. Bacon has more protein than fish and does not contain toxins such as mercury.

- Bacon is good for the brains of unborn children and has also been shown in university studies to help fight off the debilitating effects of Alzheimer's Disease and other chronic mental impairments. A research study published by scientists at the University of North Carolina shows that choline helps fetuses develop regions of the brain linked to memory.

- Bacon provides: 65% of our Recommended Daily Intake of Thiamin (Vitamin B1) as well as 47% of our Niacin (Vitamin B3), 38% of our Vitamin B12, 36% of our Zinc, 24% of our Vitamin B6, 22% of our Riboflavin (Vitamin B2), 22% of our Phosphorus, 10% of our Pantothenate, 10% of our Magnesium, 9% of our Iron.

- If you include some dairy and citrus in your bacon meal, the vitamins A, D and E work to effectively prevent conversion of "nitrates and nitrites into "nitrosamines" in the stomach, rendering them harmless to the body.

- The protein to fat balance in bacon is 4 to 1, which is one of the highest protein to fat balances found in any meat, fish or fowl.

- It is true that nitrates and nitrites are potentially unhealthy for your body, what many nutritionists fail to say is that you can easily avoid nitrates and nitrites by simply not burning / charring / over cooking bacon or by baking your bacon in the oven.

- Bacon makes you feel happy, satisfied, blissful, which greatly reduces stress and effectively relieves the negative effects of frustration and self deprivation.

- Bacon and Diets - Bacon adorns the cover of Dr. Salerno's latest diet book, "Fight Fat With Fat." An important component of the diet is the inclusion of healthy fat sources including nuts, olives, avocados, and beloved bacon.

- There are several studies that show that the Omega-3 Fatty Acids and choline found in bacon can actually protect the heart from developing problems, as well as actually help heal such anomalies, after they have occurred.

- Bacon Omega-3 can help prevent heart disease, as well as lower cholesterol, reduce inflammation and improve circulation and it does not contain mercury.

- Speaking of life expectancy, proof of bacon's health benefits come from Pearl Cantrell, a 105-year-old women who made headlines when she claimed that eating bacon is the key to her longevity. Mrs. Cantrell eats bacon every day for breakfast and sometimes at lunch. Susannah Mushatt Jones, who recently celebrated her 115th birthday, also eats bacon every day. Every morning, bacon is the first thing to disappear from her plate.

- In a study published in Nature Chemical Biology, researchers found out that the niacin (Vitamin B3) in bacon, could help you live a longer life. When the researchers fed roundworms a ton of niacin, they lived one-tenth longer than the worms that were not fed niacin.

- A company in The United Kingdom, TMI Foods has successfully found a way to use bacon grease to manufacture a powerful, low emission, minimal pollution, environmentally friendly, all-natural, bio-diesel fuel that can be used to effectively and inexpensively run anything from motor vehicles to turbines and powering generators.

Researchers from ETH Zurich find that diet including niacin-rich foods like bacon may increase life expectancy.

Choline - A study shows bacon contains a nutrient called choline which has been shown to boost memory and muscle control. When deprived of choline in their diet almost 80% of the men and postmenopausal women developed liver or muscle damage.

The study also found that young women can supply more choline, because pregnancy is a time when the body's demand for choline is highest.

Choline is particularly used to support the fetus's developing nervous system. A person can also get choline from eggs, liver, milk, chicken, and various nuts. *That proves it, bacon and eggs are good for you.*

A study was conducted on two groups of mice.
One group was fed only bacon. The other group was fed nothing.
The group being fed bacon lived much longer.

BACON RECORDS

Matthew Willer of St. Louis, Missouri and his team currently hold the world record for largest bacon explosion. This monumental tribute to bacon weighed 54.43 kilograms, or 120 pounds.

Peter Czerwinski of Mississauga, Ontario holds the records for drinking a bacon shake the fastest: 47.72 seconds. The bacon shake contained five pounds of bacon.

In 2013, Molly Schuyler from Bellevue, Nebraska, crushed the record for being the first person to eat 3 lbs of cooked bacon within less than the 5 minute time allotted. In March 2015, she polished off five pounds of bacon in a world-record 5 minutes, 21 seconds. *(She also ate two 72-ounce steaks in less than 15 minutes at a Texas BBQ in 2014.)* February 1, 2014, she won the IHOP Pancake Bowl and the bacon eating contest at the Blue Ribbon Bacon Festival in Des Moines, IA by eating 5 pounds of bacon in 3 minutes

Todd Dotson took the prize after he ate two pounds of bacon in 24 minutes, 4 seconds to win the Delphi first-ever Indiana Bacon Festival. (*He is a bit behind of the others in this category*)

Kevin Graham of Des Moines won the bacon eating contest at Blue Ribbon Bacon Fest baconmania VIII Saturday, Jan. 31, 2015. (Alas, no other details).

Matt Stonie broke the world record for consuming 182 slices (approximately six pounds) of Smithfield brand bacon in five minutes at the Daytona 500 in Florida, 2015. He smashed the previous 2010 record, held by Mark "The Human Vacuum" Lyle, by over 120 slices.

Not a bacon record, but a record with bacon helping - A trio of Canadian adventurers said they set a new record in 2013 for fastest trek across Antarctica to the South Pole, after suffering through whiteout conditions, temperatures as low as minus 40, and a steady diet of deep-fried bacon, cheese, and butter. They completed the 700-mile journey from Hercules Inlet on Antarctica's Ronne Ice Shelf to the South Pole in 33 days, 23 hours and 30 minutes.

Bacon awakens the senses as it slithers about a nubbly tongue.

BREAKFAST, BACON, AND BERNAYS

Cured pork bacon had been a staple of the European diet for centuries, but was not considered breakfast food. Until the 1920s most Americans had a relatively light breakfast.

In 1925 the Beech-Nut Packing Company (producers of everything from pork products to bubble gum.) wanted to increase consumer demand for bacon and hired Edward Bernays (1891–1995) to increase bacon sales. Austrian-born Bernays, nephew of Sigmund Freud, was quite good at using psychology to get people to buy a product or an idea. He is considered the father of public relations, spin, and propaganda. He called this scientific technique of opinion-molding the 'engineering of consent' - get indirect endorsement from a third-party, and the product, idea, or event sells itself.

Bernays turned to his agency's internal doctor and asked him whether a heavier breakfast might be more beneficial for the American public. Once he had the obvious answer, he then asked whether bacon and eggs could be considered a hearty breakfast. Again the doctor agreed.

The doctor wrote to five thousand doctors, asking them to confirm it as well. This 'study' of doctors encouraging the American public to eat a heavier breakfast 'Bacon and Eggs' was published in major newspapers and magazines of the time and reached great success. They treated this publicity stunt as a scientific study and ran story after story about how if you were not starting the day with a big plate full of bacon and eggs; you were signing your own death warrant. Beech-Nut's profits rose sharply. The all-American breakfast of bacon and eggs was born. Today, seventy percent of bacon eaten in the US is for breakfast.

Other campaigns by Bernays

Bernays staged the 1929 Easter Parade in New York City, showing models holding lit Lucky Strike cigarettes, or 'Torches of Freedom'. After the historic public event, women started lighting up more than ever before. It was through Bernays that women's smoking habits started to become socially acceptable.

Bernays once engineered a "pancake breakfast" with vaudevillians for Calvin Coolidge, in what is widely considered one of the first overt media acts for a president. He was part of the group that crafted the line, "Making the world safe for democracy." It helped sell Wilson's cause to Americans, to get them sold on entering World War I.

He worked with Procter & Gamble for Ivory-brand bar soap. The campaign successfully convinced people that Ivory soap was medically superior to other soaps. (99 and 44/100 percent pure)

His Dixie Cup campaign convinced consumers that only disposable cups were sanitary.

He helped the United Fruit Company (now Chiquita Brands International) organize a coup to overthrow the government of Guatemala, creating a better business environment for their banana fields.

Every day, millions of innocent plants are killed by vegetarians. Stop the murder.

Eat Bacon!

Sharing bacon is like being an orgasm donor.

STOP
OINKING
AND
MAKE ME
SOME BACON

Bacon Recipes

RECIPES INTRODUCTION

Bacon Recipes Rating

According to a data-mining project from Wired.com. They teamed up with FoodNetwork.com to sift through 906,539 ratings on the cooking channel's website. They searched all the recipes that fit a description, such as sandwiches and then calculated the average rating for those foods if they did not include the word bacon and only recipes that did include bacon. They found that when reviewing the data for all recipes, those with bacon rated higher.

Lada Adamic, a computer scientist at the University of Michigan also developed an algorithm for predicting how successful a recipe will be, based on the ingredient combinations used. Her team took nearly 50,000 recipes and 2 million reviews from allrecipes.com and then extracted all the ingredients, cooking methods, and nutritional profiles. With just these items, her algorithm could predict the recipe's rating with an accuracy of about 70 percent.

When she checked her data from a different recipe website, she came up with similar results to the Wired.com results. "The fact that bacon-containing recipes are rated more highly in a separate data set makes the result believable."

I could have predicted those results without science or a computer. Bacon is the all purpose food. You can mix, wrap, stuff, sprinkle, and rub it on anything to add smoky flavor goodness. Following are recipes for breakfast, main courses, snacks, and even bacon drinks. There over one hundred fifty mouthwatering recipes to tantalize your taste buds and tickle your tummy with delight.

Go ahead eat bacon and add some sizzle to your life.

How to Cook Bacon

Am sure everyone has their favorite way to cook bacon, but here are a few tips that many experts agree on.

- Let bacon sit at room temperature for about ten to fifteen minutes before cooking. It will help the fat render more quickly, so it will be crispy and not burnt.

- For microwave cooking (least desired method), line dish with multiple layers of paper towels, lay bacon in a single layer, and cover with two more layers of paper towels. Microwave on HIGH for about one minute per slice and check for doneness.

- Never cook bacon until completely done. Take it off the stove, out of the microwave, or out of the oven just before it is perfect, because it will continue to cook after it has been removed from the heat source.

- To slowly render fat without burning the meat, start cooking bacon in a cold pan.

- Cook over medium heat to let the fat render and you will have crunchier bacon.

- Add a little water to the pan to reduce splattering.

- For pan frying place a mesh or wire pan covering over the top, rather than a closed lid, which steams the bacon.

- Tongs are great to help grasp the hot slices and flip them.

- Use thick sliced bacon as often as possible for great flavor.

- Do not crowd bacon in the pan to avoid uneven cooking.

- To reduce curling, cut strips in half before cooking (kitchen shears are the perfect implement for this).

- Using a bacon press during pan frying is perfectly acceptable to keep bacon slices straight and reduce shrinkage.

- Flip bacon as you would a fine steak, only once or twice, so that it browns evenly and cooks to desired crispness.

- For oven cooking, preheat the oven to 375° and lay bacon on a foil-lined baking sheet. For crispier bacon, set a metal cooling rack on top and lay bacon on the cooling rack.

- Tear off more foil than needed and crumple, then stretch and lay in pan. Grease drains better and bacon won't stick.

- When grilling, bacon should always be cooked over indirect heat. Heat one side of grill and place bacon on the other side.

Uses for Bacon Fat

Bacon yields bacon fat or grease, which is good for many things. Many people call it bacon butter. The next time you make a batch of bacon, let the leftover fat cool a bit and then freeze it in ice cube trays. You will have spoon-sized cubes of this flavor flower whenever you want. It will last in your freezer forever.

You can also keep a jar (no straining necessary) in the refrigerator to be used as needed. It saves money and avoids waste. Jelly jars and Mason jars work well. It keeps for over a year in the refrigerator if sealed. My mother had a crock with lid and kept it on the cook top and never refrigerated it. Don't try it today as it is replenished less often and will eventually get rancid. If you are worried, use several smaller jars and discard after use, rather than topping off each time you make bacon. (*No guessing necessary, you will absolutely know when it turns rancid.*)

Use a spoonful of bacon fat anywhere you use butter, lard, olive oil, or other cooking oil. One teaspoon has just 38 calories.

- In place of butter when scrambling eggs or frying potatoes.
- Pour a tablespoonful over dog food for a special treat and to make a shiny coat.
- Adding flavor to caramelize onions.
- As the base for sautéing vegetables.
- Add to pan for cooking tater tots.
- Grease muffin tins or cast iron skillets for breads.
- Rub on chicken breasts before roasting.
- Spread on a pizza crust before adding toppings.
- Mix with milk to make milk gravy.
- Use as a base for making homemade soap.
- Add to bird feeder with peanut butter, bird seed, etc., especially during winter.
- Season cast iron pans with it.
- Spread on baking sheet to make oven fries.
- Add to water to season dried beans.
- Drizzle warmed over salad.

78

- Cook pancakes in bacon fat for extra flavor.
- Add just a bit of bacon fat when warming tortillas.
- The only way to cook popcorn is with bacon grease. It gives it a hint of bacony goodness.
- Add warm bacon fat to the top of biscuits instead of butter.
- Cornbread has always been made with bacon fat.
- Add French toast to the pan used to fry bacon for extra flavor, Also, throw a few banana slices on top at the end for more flavor.
- Make bacon scented candles.

Bacon Storage

I know it is almost heresy, but if you cannot eat all the bacon at once, you can store it.

- Once the package is open, tightly wrap or put unused bacon in an air tight container.
- To freeze unopened bacon, overwrap the store package with heavy duty foil or freezer wrapping and tightly close the wrapping around the inside package.
- Thaw frozen bacon in the refrigerator. Do not defrost in the microwave or cook from frozen.

When it comes to bacon and eggs,
chickens are involved, but pigs are committed.

All bacon is infused with sizzling saturated succulence

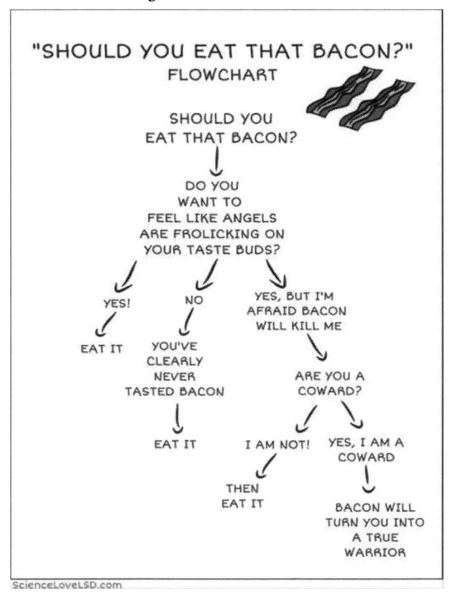

BACON BREAKFAST

There are many thousands of bacon recipes and my humble contribution will show but a small portion of them. Seventy percent of bacon is consumed at breakfast, so why not try some different recipies for a change. Train your tastebuds to enjoy new ways of being carressed.

Many recipes call for slightly cooked bacon. It means, not too crispy, because it will be cooked again as part of the recipe. This helps for even cooking of other ingredients and also reduces excess grease in the final product.

Bacon and Egg Pie

1 ½ pound thick sliced bacon, slightly cooked, roughly chopped
½ cup ketchup
¼ cup Worcestershire sauce
9 x 11 sheets frozen puff pastry, thawed and chilled
20 eggs
1 tablespoon heavy cream
Kosher salt and ground black pepper, to taste

Heat oven to 400°. Whisk together ketchup and Worcestershire in a small bowl, set aside. Using a rolling pin, roll one sheet of puff pastry on a floured work surface to form an 11 x 14 rectangle; transfer to a 9 x 12 baking pan and let excess hang over sides. Separate one of the eggs and place the egg yolk in a small bowl; stir in cream, and set egg wash aside. Place remaining egg white on top of pastry, crack rest of eggs and drop on top of pastry, spacing evenly, sprinkle all over with bacon, drizzle ketchup mixture evenly over eggs and bacon, season with salt and pepper.

Fold dough hanging over the edge of the pan back over the ingredients and brush with some of the egg wash; roll second pastry sheet into a 10 x 13 rectangle and place on top of eggs and bacon, tucking edges into sides of pan. Cut 4 slits in the top of the pastry with a paring knife, and brush with rest of egg wash. Bake until golden brown and eggs and bacon are cooked through, about one hour. Cut into squares and serve.

Bacon Breakfast Pie

Fillings
1 pound smoked thick cut bacon, slightly cooked and cut into 3/4 inch pieces

3/4 cup shredded (your choice) hard dry white cheese
1/2 pound cherry tomatoes (cut in half)
salt and black pepper to taste
1 handful salad greens

Pastry dough (makes two pies and serves about eight)
2 cups all purpose flour
1/2 teaspoon salt
1 cup chilled unsalted butter – 2 sticks (cut into pieces)
2 tablespoons half and half (or milk)
3/4 cup shredded parmesan cheese
2 large eggs (separated)

In a medium size bowl whisk one egg with half and half until thoroughly combined, set aside. In another bowl add flour, salt, and the pieces from one stick of butter. Mix until butter mixes into flour mixture. Add second stick of butter pieces and mix again until mixture becomes fine crumbles.

Pour flour mixture into the egg and half and half. Whisk to combine until the dough is damp and holds together. Combine cheese into the dough and mix until it all comes together. Separate dough into two equal pieces and wrap with plastic wrap. Place in refrigerator for at least one hour up to overnight.

Preheat oven to 350 degrees Fahrenheit.

Take out dough and let sit for 15 to 30 minutes to become workable. On a well floured surface, roll each dough piece into a circle approximately 14 inches across.

Place the dough on a parchment paper or silicon pad lined baking sheet. Sprinkle cheese evenly in the center of the dough, but leave 2 1/2 inches of empty dough around the edge of the circle. Sprinkle on bacon pieces, tomatoes, and pepper.

Fold the edges of the dough up and over the filling. Overlap each section of the dough around the edges. Sprinkle rest of cheese over top and add black pepper. Beat second egg in small bowl and brush the edges of the pie. Bake for 25 - 35 minutes. The pie is done when the crust is slightly golden brown. Remove from oven and add greens. Return to the oven for 2-3 minutes to wilt greens. Remove and serve.

Bacon Breakfast Cups

1 pound bacon, cut about in half, slightly cooked
8 eggs
1 tbsp milk
1/2 cup grated mozzarella cheese
1/2 cup hash browns separated
1/2 pound sausage

Place one strip of bacon into the hole of a muffin pan so that it sits flat inside and the edges rest over the lip of the hole. Add a second piece of bacon into the pan so that it makes a cross shape, add more to completely cover the muffin hole.

Whip eggs and place spoonful into each bacon cup. Add a layer of sausage crumbles. Add a pinch of cheese on top of sausage. Add a large spoonful of egg on top of cheese. Place a layer of hash browns on top of egg and cheese. Add another large spoonful of egg on top of hash browns. Add another pinch of cheese on top. Starting with the first (and lowest) piece of bacon placed into the cup, Fold the ends over the cheese in a circular order until they have all been folded over the top. If the ends do not lay flat, use a toothpick to pin them down.

You can mix ingredients, such as different cheeses, chopped tomatoes, chopped mushrooms, chopped spinach, chopped bell pepper, or chopped cooked ham.

Bake in oven at 400 degrees for about 25 minutes or until eggs are done and bacon is finished. Remove and serve.

Bacon Breakfast Taco

Make bacon weave drape over stiff foil so it becomes taco shaped. Cook to desired hardness and add scrambled eggs, hash browns, and shredded cheese. Put under broiler until cheese melts. remove and serve. Less mess and the children love them.

Bacon Cheese Mashed Potato Waffles

12 ounces thin sliced bacon, slightly cooked, chopped
4 tablespoons butter
1/4 cup milk
2 large eggs
2 cups mashed potatoes
1/2 cup all-purpose flour
1/2 teaspoon baking powder

1/4 teaspoon baking soda
1/2 teaspoon salt
1/2 teaspoon ground black pepper
1/4 teaspoon garlic powder
1 cup grated cheddar cheese

Melt butter in a small saucepan over medium-low heat and continue until butter begins to brown. Transfer the browned butter into a medium bowl. Whisk in milk and eggs until thoroughly combined. Add mashed potatoes and gently stir to combine.

In a small bowl, whisk together flour, baking powder, baking soda, half of chopped bacon, salt, pepper, and garlic powder. Add dry ingredients to the wet ingredients and mix until thoroughly combined.

Grease and heat waffle iron. Drop about 1/4 cup of batter per waffle into the waffle iron. Cook until golden on each side. Remove waffles and place on a cooling rack.

Just before serving the waffles, turn oven to broiler setting. Place waffles on a baking sheet and top with cheddar cheese and rest of chopped bacon. Place waffles under the broiler until cheese is melted, about 30 seconds to 1 minute. Remove and serve. Serves about 4

Bacon Chicken Pancake on a Stick

Take a deep-fried, boneless chicken breast strip on long wooden skewer, wrap it in partially cooked bacon and dip it in pancake batter. Deep fry. Remove, serve warm.

Bacon Crusted Cinnamon Rolls

The Texas State Fair has breaded, deep fried, bacon crusted cinnamon rolls. They started with a huge cinnamon roll, dipped it in a sweet pancake batter, covered it with crispy bacon crumbles, deep fried and added a pile of powdered sugar on top.

Bacon Deviled Eggs

6 slices bacon, slightly cooked, coarsely chopped
12 large eggs
1/3 cup mayonnaise
2 teaspoons Dijon mustard
Salt and pepper to taste

Strain bacon drippings through a fine-mesh sieve into a small bowl. Add melted butter if needed to measure 2 Tbsp.

Place eggs in a saucepan; add water to cover. Bring to a boil, cover, and remove from heat. Let sit for 10 minutes, drain, transfer eggs to a bowl of ice water to cool, then peel. Halve lengthwise and remove yolks.

Finely mash reserved yolks, bacon fat, mayonnaise, and mustard. Season with salt and pepper. Pipe into whites and garnish with reserved bacon.

Bacon and Egg Breakfast Pizza

Put bacon and eggs on top of smashed hash browns and fry in a pan, add cheese to top when almost done. Variation, you can also add can of crescent rolls and place them evenly under the hash browns.

Bacon Fried Wrapped Eggs

8 strips thin sliced bacon
4 soft boiled eggs
1 cup of Italian seasoning breadcrumbs
1 raw egg for topping

Wrap each egg with two strips of bacon, one horizontal and one vertical. Tuck ends in or use toothpicks so bacon stays secure and covers the entire egg.

Heat pan with oil about 1 1/2 to 2 inches deep.

Beat raw egg in a small bowl and set aside. Place bread crumbs in separate bowl and set aside.

Dip bacon wrapped eggs in raw egg. Then dip into bread crumbs until coated. Gently place into hot oil. Cook for a few minutes on each side until breadcrumbs turn brown and bacon is cooked. Serve and eat warm.

Variation – skip breading and pop bacon wrapped eggs in oven at 400 for ten to fifteen minutes, turn and cook another ten minutes. remove and serve.

Bacon Hash Brown and Egg Bake

1 pound thick cut bacon, slightly cooked, chopped
1 cup cubed ham

8 oz sliced fresh mushrooms
2 tablespoons Dijon mustard
½ teaspoon salt
½ teaspoon pepper
½ teaspoon garlic powder
¾ cup milk
12 eggs
1 package (about 2 pounds) frozen hash browns, thawed
2 cups your favorite shredded cheese
Serves 8 - 10

Drain bacon drippings, reserving one tablespoon in pan, add mushrooms; cook four minutes over medium heat, stirring occasionally. Stir in mustard, salt, and pepper.

Beat milk and eggs in a bowl and set aside.

Spray 13x9-inch baking dish with cooking spray. Spread half of hash browns in bottom, top with one cup of cheese and chopped ham. Spread remaining hash browns over cheese. Pour egg mixture on top. Cover and refrigerate four hours or overnight.

Take out mixture and let sit for one to two hours. Heat oven to 350°F. Bake 50 to 60 minutes. Sprinkle with remaining cheese and bacon. Bake 3 to 5 minutes until top is puffed and cheese is melted. Remove and serve.

Bacon Pancakes

Pour long pancakes and lay bacon on top then drizzle a bit more pancake mix on top of bacon. Cook and eat. Add maple syrup if desired.

Bacon Pancake Bites

Cook bacon until about half done, cut into 1 inch pieces, roll in pancake batter, and deep fry.

Bacon Potato Egg Breakfast Bowls

3 strips thick sliced bacon, cooked, crumbled
2 large potatoes, baked
1 Tbsp. butter
2 eggs
3 Tbsp. shredded sharp cheddar cheese
salt and pepper, to taste

Preheat oven to 350 degrees F. Spray baking sheet non-stick cooking spray.

Cut top 1/4 off of each baked potato, lengthwise. Hollow out the middle of the potato making a bowl, leaving potato thick enough to hold ingredients. (save insides to make bacon potato pancakes)

Place hollowed out baked potatoes on baking sheet and put 1/2 Tbsp. butter in bottom each. Break egg into each bowl, top with bacon, cheese, and salt and pepper.

Bake at 350 F for about 20 minutes or until egg whites are set. Remove, top with extra bacon and cheese, serve warm.

Bacon Stuffed French Toast

12 strips bacon, cut in half and cooked
½ cup real maple syrup
6 eggs
⅔ cup heavy cream
1 Tablespoon sugar
2 teaspoons ground cinnamon
2 Tablespoons vanilla extract
½ teaspoon salt, to taste
12 slices bread

In a shallow bowl, beat eggs, cream, sugar, cinnamon, vanilla, and salt, until blended.

Dip all slices of bread on one side only in egg mixture. Add four half-pieces of bacon to egg side of 6 slices, and then top with the remaining slices with egg side toward bacon, then pinch edges of each sandwich to seal. Dip both sides of each sandwich into the egg mixture and cook in an oiled or bacon greased pan over medium-high heat until nicely tanned, then flip and repeat. Remove to a plate, slice, top with butter and syrup, serve.

Bacon is the breakfast of <u>Chompians</u>!

BACON MEALS

Bacon is not just for breakfast. You can enjoy it any time of day. The following recipes include quick meal ideas to full course meals - all, of course, containing sumptuous porcine goodness of mouth watering bacon and a veritable plethora of porcineology to stimulate your bacon lust.

Bacon and Blue Cheese Encrusted Burger

Dad's Kitchen, Sacramento, Calif. - The Dad's Burger at Dad's Kitchen takes Bacon and blue cheese burgers to a whole new level. Instead of simply topping a cooked patty with crumbled blue cheese and a few strips of bacon, this patty is topped with crumbled blue cheese on both sides then wrapped in a coat of bacon and griddled to perfection.

Bacon Apple Grilled Cheese

1 package thick sliced bacon, sliced in half, cooked almost firm
1 Granny Smith apple
6 slices of sharp cheddar cheese
4 pieces of bread
Butter

Makes two sandwiches

Lay out bread then cover each with cheese, then bacon.

Core apple, slice into thin pieces. Layer apple slices on one side of bread for each sandwich.

Layer more bacon on top of apple slices, top with other cheese and bread. (layers top to bottom - cheese, bacon, apple, bacon, cheese, bacon)

Heat up pan on medium heat. Butter outside of sandwich with butter and place butter side down in pan. (Covering pan helps melt cheese faster). Flip when moderately brown and cook other side. Serve and eat.

Bacon Apple Sandwich

Spread a split baguette with honey mustard. Fill with cooked thick sliced bacon (cut in thirds for easy eating), sliced Brie, apple, lettuce. Add salt and pepper, warm, slice and serve.

Bacon Barbecue Chicken

1 pound thin sliced bacon, cut in half
15 six inch bamboo skewers
3 large boneless skinless chicken breasts
1/2 cup barbecue sauce

Soak skewers in water at least 30 minutes to prevent burning.

Cut each chicken breast in half lengthwise, then cut across to make about 10 pieces.

Heat grill to medium. Push one skewer through end of one bacon piece, then through middle of one chicken piece and back through other end of bacon piece, repeat with another bacon and chicken. Repeat to make remaining kabobs.

Place kabobs on non heated side of grill, cover grill, cook 5 minutes. Turn kabobs; brush with half of barbecue sauce. Cover; cook 5 minutes. Turn kabobs; brush with remaining sauce. Cover; cook about 1 minute longer. Remove and eat. Variation – Add colorful veggies between bacon/chicken pieces.

Bacon Beer Battered Steak Fingers

1 package thick sliced bacon, cut in half
1 medium steak, your choice
2 eggs, separated
3/4 cup beer
1 tablespoon vegetable oil
1 cup flour
Course sea salt and pepper to taste
Peanut oil for deep frying

Mix flour, seasonings, and spices together. Add in beaten the egg yolks (reserve egg whites), beer, and oil until you reach a smooth consistency. Let the batter stand for about four hours. Beat the reserved egg whites until stiff, fold the egg whites gently into the rest of the batter mixture.

Slice steak into half inch strips, season with salt and pan sear. Set aside. Once cooled, wrap each piece of steak with bacon. Pan fry the pieces over medium low until bacon is crispy.

Set aside to cool, then drop in beer batter. After dipping all of the pieces, place into 350° peanut or other oil (do not crowd), fry until golden, repeat as necessary. Remove, add pinch of coarse sea salt, eat.

Bacon Brie Apple Honey Sandwich

Top French bread with thick sliced bacon, medium slices of crunchy apples, and soft brie. Drizzle with honey to taste, serve.

Bacon Burger Supreme

This is 100% ground bacon burger topped with thick sliced chicken fried bacon, bacon aioli, bourbon bacon, red onion jam, and a fried egg, served on a bed of bacon weave. Can you say, *O R G A S M*!

Bacon Butter Turkey

6 strips bacon, uncooked, lightly chopped
4 oz salted butter, softened
6 leaves fresh sage
1 tbsp thyme leaves
1/2 tsp fresh ground pepper
1 turkey

Combine all ingredients, except turkey, in food processor and process until smooth. Scrape onto a piece of plastic wrap and shape into a log. Place in refrigerator for four or more hours to harden.

Place turkey in roasting pan. Dry with paper towels. Slice the butter into 1/4 inch rounds. Run hands between skin and meat to separate and place rounds of bacon butter under the skin. Let sit for a few minutes until the butter softens and massage to spread the butter. Bake as usual. Remove, carve, serve.

Bacon Cheese Bread Loaf

Hollow out a fresh loaf of bread, leaving a one-inch shell to serve as a bread bowl. Combine two cups of shredded Monterey Jack Cheese, one cup of shredded sharp cheddar cheese, one cup of mayonnaise, and eight strips of cooked and crumbled bacon. Ladle into bread and bake at 350 F for about an hour. Remove, slice, share.

Bacon Cheese Potato Pie

Line a pie plate with thick sliced bacon, and alternately layer thinly sliced butter brushed potatoes and cheddar cheese until full, salt, pepper, and season to taste. Close the bacon on top and bake at 350 F for about an hour and a half, check every half hour and reduce grease if necessary. Use toothpicks to hold top bacon down, if necessary. Slice like pie, share.

Bacon Country Fried with Waffles

Swine Southern Table & Bar; Coral Gables, Florida, chef Phillip Bryant gives chicken-fried bacon the center stage atop cheddar cheese waffles drizzled in honey hot sauce and bourbon maple syrup. Bryant dunks the chicken fried bacon in batter, then deep-fries it until it's golden and crisp.

Bacon Cup Pizza

1 pound thick cut bacon
1 - 2 cups shredded mozzarella
pepperoni, about 3 per cup
other pizza toppings as desired

Place one strip of bacon into the hole of a muffin pan so that it sits flat inside and the edges rest over the lip of the hole. Add a second piece of bacon into the pan so that it makes a cross shape, add more to completely cover the muffin hole, leave excess bacon hang over cups. Cook until almost done, drain excess grease.

In each cup add cheese, add 2 slices pepperoni, add other toppings if desired, add 1 slice pepperoni, add more cheese to fill cup, fold excess bacon strip edges over filling, bake at 375 F until bacon finished, cheese melted, and pepperoni bubbling. Remove, serve.

Bacon Double Dog

Wrap hot dog with bacon, hold bacon on with toothpicks, deep-fry. Cool and dip into corn batter loaded with crumbled bacon and deep-fry again. Remove, eat.

Bacon Double Wrapped Burger

Philly's PYT has introduced its new Double Bacon Wrapped Burger. The burger is made from two beef patties wrapped in four strips of bacon each. The patties are then deep-fried so that the bacon gets crispy and the juices get moist. After coming out of the fryer, the bacon-wrapped patties are seared on the grill and topped with melted cheddar cheese, then sandwiched between two toasted buttered buns with a homemade slaw consisting of lettuce, pickles, onions, mustard, mayo, garlic and vinegar. Customers can either order a single bacon-wrapped burger or the double with two wrapped patties.

Bacon Donut Burger Breakfast

Southern Californian burger chain Slater's 50/50 offers a Donut Burger on its weekend breakfast menu during regular season football.

It consists of two glazed donuts which sandwich its 50/50 half bacon, half beef burger with a sunny side up egg and cheese. It comes with a side of strawberry jelly.

Bacon Donut Dog

Krispee Kreme bacon donut dog topped with raspberry jelly. It is served at Wilmington Blue Rocks minor league baseball games.

Bacon Explosion

Bacon Explosion has just 5,000 calories per log. It is made of Kansas City style sauce rubbed Italian sausage, smoked slowly over hickory and oak wood and stuffed with bacon, then wrapped in bacon. There are variations, such as Jalapeño or Cheese.

Bacon Faux Burger

Cook one pound bacon, crumble, add two pounds grated sharp cheddar cheese. Mix cheese with bacon. Fill hamburger buns with mixture. Place bun bottoms on cookie sheet, cover with tinfoil. Bake 350 for 10 - 15 min. Add bun tops and warm them for last 5 minutes.

Bacon Grilled Cheese

Fry two grilled cheese sandwiches, cut each sandwich into four pieces, wrap each with semi cooked bacon strips. Drop them in a deep fryer for 45 seconds, or put them on a baking sheet in oven for about 15 minutes at 375° F.

A variation on this is the Bacon Weave Grilled Cheese. Cut thick cut bacon in half. Weave to about size of slice of bread. Cook until almost crisp, add thick slice of Cheddar or your favorite cheese in between two weaves, put back into oven until cheese is slightly melted.

Bacon Herb Chicken

6 slices thin cut bacon
1 chicken, cut into 8 pieces

4 cloves garlic, minced
1 finely chopped chili pepper
2 tablespoons finely chopped rosemary
2 tablespoons finely chopped thyme
Sea salt and coarsely ground pepper
1/4 cup olive oil
6 fresh bay leaves

Serves 4

Preheat oven to 375°F. Place a wire cooling rack over a baking sheet.

Place chicken in a dish with the garlic, chilies, rosemary, and thyme. Season to taste with sea salt and pepper. Drizzle olive oil over the chicken and toss evenly to coat. Use immediately or marinate up to overnight.

Place a bay leaf on top of each piece of chicken using smaller leaves for the legs. Wrap a bacon slice around each piece of chicken so that each piece is partially exposed. Arrange chicken on rack and bake 45 minutes, until bacon is crisp and chicken cooked through.

Bacon Hogs in a Blanket

8 slices of bacon, slightly cooked
8 hot dogs
2 tubes (8 count) crescent roll dough
8 hot dog length and width slices of cheese

Slice hot dogs lengthwise (leaving about 1/2 inch from each end) about 3/4 the way through, shove in one slice of cheese and one slice of bacon and close. Unroll crescent dough and break off pieces in groups of two, pinch seams together to make one big dough.

Roll dog/cheese/bacon in dough, stretching to fit. A toothpick can be used to make sure bacon and cheese stay in place. Depending on the size of dogs and dough, some dog ends might extend outside of dough. Place on foil lined cookie sheet and cook according to directions on the crescent roll package. Remove, let slightly cool to eliminate hot cheese burn, serve.

Bacon Lettuce Tomato Monster

One pound of thick sliced cooked bacon on toasted buttered Italian bread loaf, sans lettuce and tomato. *This is on my ToDo list.*

Bacon Mac and Cheese

Prepare a standard casserole dish and add a pound of penne pasta and a pound of shredded cheddar. Slightly cook and rough chop a pound of thick sliced bacon. Add the bacon and cover with more cheese, let it brown in the oven for about 30 minutes. Variation - Use fontina, provolone, parmesan, applewood bacon, and breadcrumbs.

Bacon Meatballs

Pulse 6 ounces cooked bacon in a food processor. Add 1 cup breadcrumbs, 1/2 cup each chopped onion, chopped parsley, grated Parmesan, 4 garlic cloves, 2 eggs, and salt and pepper to taste. Pulse to combine. Form into small balls. Brown in a skillet with olive oil or bacon grease, then simmer in tomato sauce until cooked through.

Bacon Monte Cristo Sandwich

8 slices bacon, thick cut, cooked and cut in half
8 sliced bread
8 slices deli ham
8 slices cheese
butter, softened
3 eggs
1/4 cup milk
salt and pepper to taste

Preheat oven to 400 degrees F. Lay out 8 slices of bread, cover each slice with butter. Lay a slice of cheese on each of four slices of bread, then ham on top of each slice of cheese, then 4 bacon halves on each of the four slices. On other 4 slices reverse and put bacon, ham, then cheese. Put 4 slices together with other 4 slices. (layers top to bottom - cheese, ham, bacon, cheese, ham, bacon)

Wrap together with plastic wrap and refrigerate for at least 30 minutes to 1 hour. Combine eggs and milk in a bowl. Heat a griddle or large frying pan over medium-high heat and generously butter it. Unwrap the sandwiches and dip each in egg batter to coat evenly. Place each on buttered griddle or pan to cook. Turn once and then cover until golden brown and hot, about 5 minutes total. Remove, slice in half diagonally, douse with powdered sugar and serve with jelly for dipping.

Bacon Mushroom Gravy and Jagerschnitzel

1/2 pound bacon, chopped
1 1/2 pounds pork loin, cut into 6-ounce portions
1 cup all-purpose flour
1 tablespoon salt
1 teaspoon ground black pepper
1 teaspoon granulated garlic
1 teaspoon paprika
1 egg
1/2 cup milk
2 teaspoons mustard
1 cup crushed unsalted crackers
1 cup bread crumbs
1/2 diced yellow onion, approximately 1/2 cup
2 cups sliced button mushrooms
1/4 cup red wine
Olive oil, for frying
2 cups beef stock
2 tablespoons butter, room temperature

Preheat oven to 350 degrees F. Pound pork slices between sheets of plastic wrap to 1/4-inch thickness. In a shallow medium bowl, mix together 3/4 cup flour with salt, pepper, garlic and paprika. In another shallow medium bowl, combine egg, milk and mustard. In another medium bowl, combine cracker and bread crumbs. Dredge pork slices first in flour, then in egg wash, then in crumbs. Let set on a baking sheet fitted with a cooling rack for 5 minutes.

Cook bacon until done. Remove from pan, drain. In same pan with bacon fat, add onions and sauté for 3 minutes. Add mushrooms and continue sautéing for 2 minutes. Stir in 1/4 cup flour. Cook flour to make roux until light brown, about 2 minutes. Add wine and cook for 3 minutes, reducing by 1/3, then add stock. Continue cooking to reduce by 1/3 again. Season with salt and pepper. Keep warm.

Heat 1/4-inch oil in thick sauté pan or cast iron skillet to 350 degrees F. Cook pork evenly on both sides, about 5 minutes for the first side, 3 to 4 minutes for the second. Remove, add butter to sauce, stirring until it has melted, cover pork with sauce, sprinkle with chopped bacon, and serve. Serves 4 - 6

Bacon Peanut Butter Maple Fudge

12 strips maple-smoked bacon
1 1/2 cups semisweet chocolate chips
1/2 cup peanut butter chips
14-ounces sweetened condensed milk
4 tablespoons unsalted butter
1/2 teaspoon maple extract

Coat an 8-inch-square pan with cooking spray. Cook bacon, drain, and chop. Reserve 2 of the chopped slices for garnish.

Combine all ingredients except bacon in a medium saucepan over medium-low heat. Stir continuously until chips and butter are melted, and mixture is thick and smooth. Remove from heat. Stir in bacon.

Pour into prepared pan, sprinkle the reserved chopped bacon on top and lightly press. Cover with aluminum foil and chill in the refrigerator until firm, at least 4 hours or overnight. Slice into squares, serve at room temperature.

Bacon PBJ and Apple

8 slices slightly cooked bacon
1/4 cup peanut butter
2 tbsp. apple butter
4 sandwich wraps/tortillas
2 tbsp. apple jelly
1 apple

In a small bowl, use a spoon to mix peanut butter and apple butter together.

Lay the wraps on a surface and spread peanut/apple butter mixture equally on 1/2 of each wrap. Spread the apple jelly evenly on the other half of each.

Place four or five slices of apple on the peanut-butter mixture and two strips of bacon on top of the apples. Fold the tortillas into wrap sandwiches, serve.

Bacon Peanut Butter and Jelly

Add 4 half slices of cooked bacon to center of peanut butter and jelly sandwich, butter outside of sandwich and fry in pan like a grilled cheese. Remove, serve warm. *These are amazing!*

Bacon Perfect Meal

1 pound thick sliced bacon
2 cups cooked crumbled bacon
1 pound thin sliced bacon
2 tablespoons cooked chopped bacon
1 dash bacon sauce
1 pound of favorite cheese, grated or sliced

Make bacon weave of thick sliced bacon, make bacon weave of thin sliced bacon, partially cook thick slice bacon weave, take out and place other ingredients on evenly, lay thin slice bacon weave on top, turn oven to broil and cook until cheese bubbles and bacon sizzles, Remove, eat and let it tantalize your taste buds. *If possible, save a few pieces to put in your pocket and make women love you.*

Bacon Pork Tenderloin

8 slices smoked bacon, slightly cooked
3 tablespoons apple butter
2 tablespoons honey
1/3 teaspoon ground allspice
¼ teaspoon chili powder
1 whole pork tenderloin

Preheat oven to 325 degrees F. Spray a broiler pan with cooking spray. Mix apple butter, honey, allspice, and chili powder in a small bowl.

Wrap tenderloin in 4 slices of slightly cooked bacon and secure with toothpicks. Brush half the apple butter mixture over bacon and wrap tenderloin with remaining slices of bacon. Brush remaining apple butter mixture over the meat. Place tenderloin on broiling pan.

Bake until apple butter mixture has baked into a glaze and a meat thermometer inserted into the thickest part of the tenderloin reads at least 145 degrees, about 30 minutes.

Bacon Potato Pancakes

Cook 4 slices bacon, drain, and chop. Shred 2 washed russet potatoes; squeeze dry. Mix in bacon, and salt, and pepper. Cook in the bacon drippings on medium high until crisp, about 7 minutes per side.

Bacon Roasted Potatoes

Coat bottom of a sheet pan with softened bacon grease and toss potatoes to coat them evenly. Add salt, pepper, garlic, and rosemary to taste. Cook in 425°F oven until crispy.

Bacon Rosemary Meatballs

4 strips bacon
10 ounces ground beef
6 ounces sweet italian pork sausage, skin removed
4 ounces hot italian pork sausage, skin removed
1 1/2 cups panko breadcrumbs
1 large egg, lightly beaten
2 garlic cloves, minced
1 teaspoon finely chopped fresh rosemary or 1/2 teaspoon dried
1 tablespoon lemon juice
1 tablespoon olive oil
coarse salt and ground pepper to taste

In a large bowl, mix beef, Italian sausage, panko bread crumbs, egg, garlic, rosemary, lemon juice, 1/2 teaspoon coarse salt, and 1/4 teaspoon pepper. Form into one inch meatballs.

Fry bacon, and save the grease. Line a glass pan with the bacon grease and 1 teaspoon of olive oil, and add meatballs. Bake for approximately 25 minutes at 350 degrees F. remove and serve with your favorite red sauce.

Bacon Sirloin Burger

1 pound bacon chopped
1 pound ground sirloin
1 tablespoon Worcestershire sauce
1-1/4 c Soft bread crumbs
1 egg
½ tsp salt
¼ tsp pepper
2 tablespoons flour

Combine bacon with sirloin, Worcestershire, bread crumbs, egg, salt and pepper and blend well. Form 4 to 6 patties and coat with flour lightly. Grill as usual or fry in pan with vegetable oil or bacon grease. Add more bacon and cheese on top, warm until cheese melts, drool, remove, serve hot between warmed hamburger buns.

Bacon Slices and Baked Potato

Cut potato lengthwise to make flat bottom for cooking and slice, not too thin and not all the way through.

Insert half slice of thin cut bacon between each slice. Drizzle melted butter and pinch of sea salt over top.

Bake 375 about 45 minutes. Add grated Cheddar cheese over top and back into oven about 5 minutes until cheese is runny. Remove, serve.

Bacon Spiral Barbecue Hot Dogs

Spiral slice hot dog, stick long skewer through and separate spirals, weave thin sliced bacon around between each opening, grill. Add barbecue sauce just before done. Remove from heat, remove skewer, stick dog in bun, sprinkle with cheese, serve.

Bacon Turkey

Wrap thick sliced bacon to completely cover turkey before cooking, cook turkey as usual. Variation - warm up your leftover turkey in the oven with a few strips of bacon draped on top. It enhances the flavor. Partially cook the bacon first, so you do not overheat the leftover turkey.

Bacon Turbaconducken

Chicken stuffed in duck, stuffed in a 15 lb. turkey, all packaged in pork bacon. The bacon isn't just on the outside. The chicken pieces are wrapped in it, then the duck is bundled in bacon, and then the turkey is covered in more bacon.

Bacon Wrapped Burger

Philly's PYT has introduced their new Double Bacon-Wrapped Burger made from two beef patties wrapped in four strips of bacon each. The patties are then deep-fried so that the bacon gets crispy and the juices get moist. After coming out of the fryer, the bacon-wrapped patties are seared on the grill and topped with melted cheddar cheese, then sandwiched between two toasted buttered buns with a homemade slaw consisting of lettuce, pickles, onions, mustard, mayo, garlic and vinegar.

Bacon Wrapped Chicken Tenderloins

1 pound thin sliced bacon
2 pounds chicken tenderloins
1/3 cup raw honey
1 tbsp Dijon mustard
2 tsp fresh chopped thyme
1 tsp smoked paprika
juice from half a lemon
1 tbsp orange zest
½ tsp ground black pepper
pinch of salt

Preheat oven to 350 F. Wrap each piece of chicken with a piece of bacon. Place on a cookie tray lined with aluminum foil.

Mix together honey, mustard, paprika, lemon juice, zest, salt and pepper in a small bowl. Use a pastry brush or ladle to coat the top of bacon wrapped chicken.

Bake in oven for about 12 minutes then flip the chicken over, brush the remaining glaze on the other side and bake for another 12 minutes or until the chicken is done. Remove, serve.

Bacon Weave Grilled Cheese

Fry two weaves of bacon until slightly done, insert thick slab of cheese between, continue cooking until cheese melts, remove, eat.

Bacon Weave Pizza

One pound thick slice bacon weave, top with pizza sauce, mozzarella cheese, Italian sausage, and pepperoni, cook at 400 degrees F about 20 to 25 minutes. Remove, serve. *Ciao bella!*

Bacon Weave Taco Mac and Cheese

Make two bacon weave taco shells and fill with warm macaroni and cheese between them, serve.

Bacon Wrapped BBQ Shrimp

12 strips smoked bacon
1 small jalapeño pepper
1/2 cup barbecue sauce
4 bamboo skewers soaked in water
12 medium-size fresh uncooked shrimp

Preheat oven 350° F. Shell shrimp leaving tail intact. Make a shallow cut lengthwise down the back of each shrimp; wash, and de-vein.

Remove seeds from pepper and cut into 12 slivers, then, make a shallow cut into the underside of each shrimp and insert a piece of pepper.

Wrap each shrimp with a bacon strip. Thread 3 bacon/shrimp bundles onto each skewer, leaving a small space between bundles. Bake for 10 minutes until done, but not crispy.

Baste with barbecue sauce. Grill or pan sear, uncovered, for 4 to 5 minutes. Turn, baste and grill an additional 4 to 5 minutes, or until bacon is crisp and shrimp has turned pink. Remove and serve with additional barbecue sauce.

Bacon Wrapped Fried Mac & Cheese

15 slices thin sliced bacon
Flour
2 eggs, beaten
Plain bread crumbs
Mac and Cheese cooked, chilled in refrigerator overnight, and cut into 15 squares
Peanut oil, for frying

Heat peanut oil to 350 degrees F. Wrap each square with 1 strip of bacon, and fasten with toothpick. Dredge each square in flour then egg and then bread crumbs to coat. Fry for about 3 minutes until golden brown.

Bacon Wrapped Pulled Pork Grilled Cheese Sandwich

Wrap at least eight strips of thick sliced bacon around each of two sandwiches of bread, encasing pulled pork and shredded cheese. Fry or bake until bacon is done. Remove, eat.

Bacon Wrapped Grilled Cheese

from buzzfeed

Lay 5 slices thin cut bacon with long edges barely overlapping, to match size of bread. Make sandwich with two slices of bread and thick cheese. Lay sandwich on bacon. Wrap five more slices of bacon in the opposite direction. Sear both sides in frying pan, then stand up and sear edges. Remove, eat.

Bacon Wrapped Teriyaki Chicken Skewers

8 oz. thin sliced bacon, cut in half
1 pound boneless skinless chicken breasts or thighs
1 large can pineapple chunks
Teriyaki sauce
kebab skewers soaked in water for about 20 minutes to keep from burning

Separate bacon strips and lay on foil then place in refrigerator (to make it easier to handle). Count bacon pieces and cut chicken into equal number of bite-sized pieces.

Drain pineapple, wrap a piece of bacon around each chicken piece, secure with skewer, top with a chunk of pineapple, repeat if skewer is long enough, then place into 9 x 13 baking dish. Pour Teriyaki sauce over top of completed skewers, reserving about 1/4 cup. Marinate in refrigerator for at least 2 hours, but not overnight.

Preheat grill to medium high, place skewers on grill and baste with reserved Teriyaki sauce. Cook about 7 minutes and flip. Baste again and cook another 7 minutes. If cooking in oven, preheat oven to 400 and bake about 20 minutes, turning once to baste. Remove, serve, or can be put in crock pot and served warm all day.

Baconator Dumpling

Just saw this on the web, peanut butter baconator dumpling. Put a gob of peanut butter and some cooked chopped bacon in a potato dumpling and deep fry. *Am searching to see if the cook is a long lost relative.*

True Bacon Burger

A friend of mine, Chris Joles sent this one to me. Geekdad, from the eponymous web site, made a burger of 100% ground bacon and added an egg to help bind it. He cooked it under the broiler so the drippings didn't mess up his grill.

His conclusions, try one, do not make it too big, use uncured bacon to reduce the salt content, eat it with a strong beer, enjoy. *I agree.*

John Mascitti, Baconista

Gold is the bacon of precious metals.

BACON SIDES AND SNACKS

Of course bacon goes with everything. It also enhances everything. Bacon is the food that makes other food taste good. It is not just a food, but also a condiment and a flavor rejuvenator. My personal favorite it the bacon wrapped bacon - tiny luscious bacon bites to pop in your mouth any time of day or night.

Bacon Chocolate Chip Cookies

adapted from nytimes.com

8 slices of bacon, cooked and chopped
1 3/4 cups flour
1/2 teaspoon baking soda
3/4 teaspoon baking powder
1/2 cup plus 2 tablespoons room temp. or 2 T bacon grease
1/2 cup plus 1 tablespoon sugar
1/2 cup plus 2 tablespoons brown sugar
1 egg
1 teaspoon vanilla extract
1/2 cup dark chocolate, chopped
sea salt to taste

Sift flour, baking soda, baking powder into a bowl and set aside. Cream butter and sugars until light and fluffy, mix in egg, stir in vanilla. Add dry ingredients and mix until combined, add in chocolate and bacon. Refrigerate for 24 to 36 hours.

Preheat oven to 350 F. Line a baking sheet with parchment paper, scoop 9 even mounds of dough onto the baking sheet leaving ample space between cookies. Sprinkle cookies with a touch of sea salt. Bake until golden brown but still soft, 18-20 minutes. Cool on sheet for 10 minutes then move to rack to cool a bit more. Remove, serve.

Bacon and Nuts

Beat 1 egg white until frothy; mix with 2 cups mixed nuts, pinch of cayenne, 2 tablespoons brown sugar, 6 slices cooked, crumbled bacon. Bake at 325 degrees F, 10 minutes. Remove, serve.

Bacon Apple Bourbon Caramel

1 pound bacon
4 medium sized red apples, peeled
2 cups brown sugar
1 cup butter
3/4 cup corn syrup
1 cup milk
1/4 cup bourbon
1 tsp. vanilla extract

Wrap each apple tightly with overlapping slices of bacon, starting from the bottom up until completely covered. Secure final strip of bacon with a toothpick. Place bacon wrapped apples on the cool side of the grill, cover, and allow them to cook for approximately 20 minutes until the bacon is brown and crisp and the apple has softened. Remove, insert popsicle sticks in to the top of each apple, and allow them to cool in fridge.

Heat the brown sugar, butter, corn syrup, milk, bourbon, and vanilla extract in a small saucepan over medium heat. Insert a candy thermometer into the saucepan making sure that it doesn't touch the bottom. Allow the mixture to simmer until it reaches a temperature of 245 degrees. Remove from the heat and stir for 2-3 minutes until the bubbles subside and the caramel has thickened slightly.

Insert more toothpicks to keep bacon in place and dip apples into caramel so that the bottom half is covered. Remove, set on a foil covered plate to cool, serve.

Bacon Apple Crisp

From Bacon Today web site

Apple Crisp Filling:
8 slices bacon, cooked, chopped
4 Granny Smith apples
1/4 cup granulated sugar
1 teaspoons ground cinnamon
1/2 teaspoon ground nutmeg
1/2 teaspoon ground ginger
1 tablespoon lemon juice

Gingersnap Topping:
1 tablespoon cold bacon grease
3/4 cup flour
1/3 cup granulated sugar
1/3 cup light brown sugar, packed
1/4 teaspoon kosher salt
1 cup finely ground Gingersnap cookies
7 tablespoons cold unsalted butter, diced

Preheat the oven to 350 degrees F. Butter or grease a medium sized baking dish. In a small bowl, mix sugar and spices. Peel, core, and cut the apples into wedges. In a large bowl, combine apple slices, lemon juice, and sugar/spice mixture. Coat apple wedges, add chopped bacon, pour the apple mixture into the buttered dish.

In a medium bowl, combine flour, sugar, brown sugar, salt, and gingersnap cookies, blend in cold butter until crumbly, then gently fold in bacon grease. Sprinkle the mixture evenly over apples.

Place on a sheet pan and bake for about 40 minutes to an hour until the top is brown and the apple are bubbly. Remove, serve warm. If desired, add ice cream with a drizzle of maple syrup.

Bacon Apple Pie

DC's Birch & Barley, GBD and Buzz Bakery, likes to mix six to eight slices of chopped, crispy bacon into to her favorite apple filling and swap two ounces of bacon fat for the same amount of butter in the crust.

Bacon Apple Cake

Cake
8 strips bacon, with 2 strips reserved for garnish
2 cups all-purpose flour
2 teaspoons baking soda
1/4 teaspoon salt
1/4 teaspoon cinnamon
6 tablespoons unsalted butter at room temperature
2/3 cups sugar
2 large eggs
3/4 teaspoon maple extract
3/4 cups buttermilk
1 cup peeled, diced Granny Smith apples
1/2 cup pecans, coarsely chopped

Glaze
6 tablespoons confectioners' sugar
3 tablespoons maple syrup
Dash of cinnamon
Makes 16 (2-inch) square pieces

Preheat oven to 350 degrees F. Butter, or coat with cooking spray, an 8-inch-square pan.

In a large skillet over medium heat, cook bacon, turning several times, until browned and crisp, 6 to 8 minutes. Transfer to a paper towel-lined plate to drain. Chop. Reserve 2 of the chopped slices for garnish.

In a large bowl, combine flour, baking soda, salt, and cinnamon. In another large bowl, using an electric mixer, cream the butter and sugar. Add eggs and maple extract, and beat at medium speed until light. Reduce speed to low and add buttermilk and beat until blended. Add the dry ingredients; beat until mixed and the flour is dissolved. Stir in the apples, pecans, and bacon.

Pour the batter into pan and smooth top with a spatula. Bake for 40 to 45 minutes, or until the cake is golden brown and a cake tester inserted into center comes out clean. Transfer the cake to a rack and cool for 10 minutes, unmold and replace on rack.

In a small bowl, whisk confectioners' sugar, maple syrup and cinnamon until smooth. Using a spoon, drizzle the icing in a back-and-forth motion across the cake. Sprinkle with the reserved chopped bacon. Allow to set for at least 30 minutes before slicing. Can be stored on countertop for one to two days, then refrigerated in an airtight container.

Bacon Avocado Fries

4 slices thin cut bacon, cut in half
1 large avocado
1 egg
1 tablespoon water
1 cup breadcrumbs
1/2 cup flour
1/4 teaspoon cayenne pepper
Salt and pepper, to taste
1-inch layer of oil in frying pan

Peel, pit, and slice avocado into 8 equal wedges. Place wedges on a dish, cover with plastic wrap and freeze for 20 minutes. In a shallow dish, whisk together egg and water. Place breadcrumbs and flour into two separate dishes. Season the flour with cayenne, salt, and pepper.

Once the avocados have chilled, take each wedge and dredge in flour. Shake off excess and dip into egg wash. Roll wedges in breadcrumbs. Take a 1/2 slice of bacon and wrap it around each wedge, secure with toothpicks. Place back onto plate and freeze for another 10 minutes. Fill a heavy bottom pan with 1 inch of oil and heat until the oil reaches 350 degrees F. Fry avocado slices for 3-4 minutes, turning as they become golden. Remove, salt, serve.

Bacon Baklava

Sweet Kentucky pig and sweeter local honey, is prepared by Brian Logsdon, pastry chef of the English Grill at Louisville's Brown Hotel.

1 1/2 pounds sliced bacon, cooked, crumbled
1 cup whole blanched almonds, toasted and coarsely chopped
3/4 cup coarsely chopped dates
1 package phyllo dough
10 tablespoons unsalted butter, melted
1 1/2 cups sugar
1 cup pure maple syrup
1/2 cup water
2 tablespoons bourbon
Finely grated zest of 1/2 orange

Preheat oven to 400 degrees. Finely chop crumbled bacon, almonds, dates in food processor.

Butter a 9-by-13-inch metal baking pan. Lay a sheet of phyllo in the pan; trim the edges to fit and brush with butter. Repeat with 4 more phyllo sheets and butter. Spread 1 cup of the filling evenly over the phyllo. Repeat this layering of 5 phyllo sheets and bacon filling two more times. Top with 5 buttered phyllo sheets, buttering the top well.

With a small, sharp knife, cut the baklava into diamonds. Bake the baklava for 10 minutes at 400 degrees F. Then lower temperature to 325 degrees and bake for 1 hour longer, or until nicely browned.

Combine sugar, maple syrup, water, bourbon, and orange zest in a saucepan and bring to a boil. Simmer for 5 minutes, then let cool to room temperature. Pour the cooled syrup over the hot baklava and let stand uncovered at room temperature overnight. Slice and serve. Makes about 35 pieces.

Bacon Balls Deep Fried

Moist chocolate cake is mixed with creamy chocolate frosting, maple syrup, and bacon pieces. The mixture is then rolled into balls and deep fried. The hot cake balls are dusted with powdered sugar, drizzled with chocolate and maple syrup, then finished with more bacon crumbles. Texas State fair, 2014.

Bacon Banana Bread

Stir 1/2 cup cooked, crumbled bacon into your favorite banana bread batter before baking.

Bacon Banana on a Stick

12 slices of bacon, cooked, coarsely chopped
8 medium bananas (as straight as possible)
Sea salt to taste
12 ounces semi sweet chocolate
8 wooden popsicle sticks or skewers

Peel bananas and carefully insert a popsicle stick or skewer into bottom end of each banana, halfway up. Arrange bananas on a baking sheet or wax paper and freeze until firm but not frozen hard, about 1 hour.

Melt chocolate in a deep metal bowl set over a saucepan of barely simmering water, stirring occasionally, until smooth. Remove bowl of chocolate from pan.

Working with 1 banana at a time, set banana in bowl and coat most of banana evenly in chocolate by spooning it on and smoothing it with the back of the spoon.

Immediately add pinch of course sea salt to chocolate covering, sprinkle bacon over chocolate coating while chocolate is still wet, then return coated banana to wax paper or baking sheet. Refreeze or chill to firm up chocolate.

Coated bananas can be kept frozen for days if covered with plastic wrap. *Note: you can cut bananas in half to make 16 portions.*

Bacon Banana with Peanut Butter (Bacon Elvis)

Slice 1/4 inch pieces of banana (like thick coins), add dollop of peanut butter, sprinkle with finely chopped bacon, add two to three grains Kosher salt. Serve and eat. *Caution, make lots. This goes quickly. Best if served slightly chilled.*

Bacon Banana Split

Add course crumbled bacon on top of a banana split for extra crunch and saltiness.

Bacon Barbecue

1 pound thick sliced bacon
Your favorite BBQ sauce for marinade
wooden skewers

Open package, separate bacon strips and put into a one gallon zip top bag. Pour the marinade over the bacon and mix thoroughly.

Remove air from the bag, seal it and store in refrigerator for at least 4 hours or overnight. Soak wooden skewers in water at least 20 minutes.

Thread the skewers through the meaty length of the bacon. Heat up half of grill. Place bacon on the unheated side of the grill and cook for 5 to 8 minutes, flip and cook for another 5 to 8 minutes. Remove and serve. You can also use Ranch Dressing or heat some cheese for dipping.

Bacon Bouquet

From Bacon Bacon, San Francisco - Five Strips of Bacon with 100% Maple Syrup Drizzle.

Cook several slices thick cut bacon until rigid. Wrap with butcher or other wax lined paper, leaving top half exposed. Present to your BFF and watch their eyes well up with delight. *If she shares with you, marry her, if not, dump her or you will never get any more bacon.*

Bacon Bourbon Caramel Popcorn

From the 2015 Kentucky Derby menu

1/2 - 1 lb thick cut bacon, cooked and chopped
5 quarts plain popped corn
1 cup butter
2 cups brown sugar
1/2 cup light corn syrup or 1/2 cup maple syrup
1 teaspoon sea salt
1/2 teaspoon baking soda
3 ounces Woodford Reserve Bourbon

Preheat oven to 250° F. Melt one cup of butter over medium heat. Mix in brown sugar, corn syrup, sea salt, and stir until boiling at the edges. Lower the heat slightly and let boil until the caramel is 250°. Remove from heat and add the baking soda and bourbon. Once fully incorporated, stir in the bacon.

Divide the popcorn into two very lightly greased roasting pans and coat with the caramel. Mix well and then put the popcorn into the preheated oven for about 45 minutes to an hour, mixing every 10-15 minutes so the kernels of popped corn is coated in bourbon bacon coating.

Once done, pour onto parchment paper or wax paper to cool. Break into pieces and serve.

Bacon Brittle

Boil 2 cups sugar and 1 cup water in a saucepan without stirring, for 8 to 10 minutes. Stir in 1 cup peanuts, 6 slices cooked, crumbled bacon, 1 tablespoon butter, a pinch each of cayenne and cinnamon. Spread on a greased baking sheet to harden.

Bacon Breadsticks

1/2 pound thin sliced bacon
One package Pillsbury original breadsticks
Grated Parmesan cheese
Garlic salt to taste
3 tablespoons olive oil

Preheat the oven to 400 degrees F. Twist each raw breadstick with a slice of bacon. Brush with olive oil, shake on Parmesan, garlic and bake for 20 minutes.

Bacon Brownies

Bacon enhances the sweetness and intensifies the brownie's rich chocolate flavor and adds depth.

1/2 cup bacon grease
2 eggs
1/2 cup coffee
1 cup maple syrup
1 cup oat flour
1 cup cocoa powder
1 tsp salt
1 tsp baking soda

Heat bacon grease until almost melted, pour into a large mixing bowl, stir in maple syrup and coffee. Whisk eggs in a separate bowl and combine, stir in cocoa powder, oat flour, salt, and baking soda.

Bake in a shallow baking dish or ramekins for 15-20 minutes at 250 F. Remove, let brownies sit for 15 minutes or refrigerate to cool, serve.

Bacon Brownie Oreos

1 pound thin sliced bacon
1 package brownie batter Oreos
oil for frying
toothpicks

Wrap each Oreo with one slice bacon. Wrap once around, then continue wrap in the other direction, secure with toothpick through filling, fry in shallow oil on medium heat. Drool, remove, eat warm.

Bacon Brussels Sprouts

3 strips thick cut bacon, chopped
1 pound small brussels sprouts (thick ends trimmed)
2 tablespoons maple syrup
2 teaspoons apple cider vinegar
2 teaspoons grainy mustard

Preheat stove to 500 degrees F, along with empty baking pan. Remove pan from oven and toss on the chopped bacon pieces, spread evenly. Place back into oven and cook for 10 minutes.

While the bacon is cooking, mix the maple syrup, vinegar, and mustard in a small container and set aside.

Remove bacon pan from oven, add brussels sprouts and stir so they get coated in the bacon fat. Return pan to oven to cook for 15 minutes. Remove pan from oven and pour maple syrup mixture evenly over bacon and sprouts. Serve warm.

Bacon Butter

Cook 2 slices bacon in a skillet; drain and chopped fine. Blend 1 stick softened butter with the drippings and 2 tablespoons maple syrup. Stir in the chopped bacon. Refrigerate and use as desired.

Bacon Candy Bits

Preheat oven to 375 degrees. Place 1 pound of thick-cut bacon, sliced in half, in single layer on a foil-lined rimmed baking sheet. Bake until crispy, about 20 minutes.

Combine ¾ cup beer, 1 cup maple syrup, 2 tablespoons black pepper, and 1 teaspoon salt in a medium saucepan.

Bring the glaze to a simmer over medium heat, stirring often, until liquid is reduced by half to syrup consistency, about 20 minutes. Brush a thick layer of glaze over the bacon and bake until caramelized, 8-10 minutes. Let cool on a wire rack about 5 minutes or until glaze hardens. Remove and serve.

Bacon Candy (Hot)

One pound thick sliced bacon cut in half, 5 tablespoons brown sugar, dash of Cayenne pepper, dash of chile powder, black pepper, Mix dry ingredients, coat bacon (Hand rub the mixture on bacon to ensure a good coating) Bake at 350 degrees until desired crispiness, about twenty minutes. Remove and serve.

Bacon Cheddar Fries

Had to add this one sent by a friend, Jim Sheppard. Cover cooked fries with semi-cooked chopped bacon and grated cheese, place on baking sheet under broiler until cheese melts. Remove, eat.

Bacon Cheese Bites

1 pound bacon, slightly cooked, finely chopped
8 ounces cream cheese, softened
1 pinch ground black pepper, to taste
2 (8 ounce) packages refrigerated crescent roll dough

Preheat oven to 350 degrees F. In a mixing bowl, combine cream cheese, bacon crumbles, and pepper. On a lightly floured surface, unroll the crescent rolls lengthwise and form into a long rectangle. Spread cream cheese mixture on the dough. Starting with the long edge of the rectangle, roll dough into a long, thin roll. Slice the roll into 1/4 inch thick pieces. Place rolls on a lightly greased baking sheet. Bake in preheated oven for 15 minutes, or until brown. Remove, serve.

Bacon Cheese Rollups

12 slices thin bacon, slightly cooked
4 slices bread

4 slices American or Velveeta cheese
1 1/2 tablespoons melted butter, or bacon grease

Cut off crusts from four slices of bread. Flatten the bread then place one slice of cheese and 4 slices bacon on each slice of bread. Cut of ends of bacon too long to fit into bread and enjoy while finishing recipe. Roll up tightly with bacon and cheese inside. Melt 1-1/2 tablespoons butter or bacon grease in a skillet over medium heat. Add rollups, seam sides down and cook until golden brown, turning occasionally, 4 to 5 minutes. If the roll ups start to open up use tongs to squeeze together or add toothpicks. Remove, slice into 3/4 inch slices, serve.

Bacon Cheese Hash Browns

2 pounds thin sliced bacon, slightly cooked, chopped
1 28 ounce or larger bag frozen hash browns
4 cups shredded cheese
2 tablespoons melted butter
Salt to taste
Garlic powder to taste

In a 9 x 12 casserole pan, place hash browns mixed with half of bacon, drizzle with melted butter, lightly salt, bake at 400 degrees about 20 - 30 minutes or until slightly golden brown.

Sprinkle on garlic powder, then add cheese and rest of bacon, bake at 375 for about 15 minutes or until cheese is melted. Remove and serve.

Bacon Cheese Puff Pastry

4 slices thin cut bacon, lightly cooked and cut in half
One 15-by-10-inch sheet puff pastry, cut into eight 3-inch rounds
4 string cheeses, halved
1 egg, beaten

Preheat the oven to 350 degrees F. Lay each puff pastry round on a baking sheet, spaced evenly apart. Wrap each string cheese half in a bacon half and then place, seam side down, in the center of each round. Taking the edges of the puff pastry, stretch and fold over the bacon-wrapped string cheese and seal tightly. For additional kick, add a pinch of cayenne. Brush each string cheese puff with a little egg wash and bake in the oven until puffed golden brown, about 25 minutes. Remove, serve. *Serves one, unless married, then two.*

Bacon Cheese Potatoes

1/2 pound thin sliced bacon, cut in half
2 medium onions, diced
4 medium potatoes, thinly sliced
1/2 pound cheddar cheese, thinly sliced

Line crock pot with foil, leaving enough to cover potatoes when finished. Layer half each of bacon, onions, potatoes, and cheese in crock pot. Season to taste and dot with butter. Repeat layers of bacon, onions, potatoes and cheese. Dot with butter. Cover with remaining foil. Cover and cook on low for 10-12 hours. Remove and serve.

Bacon Cheese Roll Weave

Weave thin sliced bacon and slightly cook, lay generous amount of favorite hard cheese and roll up, warm in oven until cheese slightly melts. Remove, cut in two inch slices. *Great for parties and game day, especially with warm barbecue sauce for dipping.*

Bacon Cheeseburger Balls

Use cupcake pan and place one strip of thick sliced bacon into the hole of the muffin pan so that it sits flat inside and the edges rest over the lip of the hole and add more crossed bacon to completely cover the muffin hole.

Add hamburger with center pushed in, fill with cheese of choice, press hamburger back enclosing cheese, fold bacon back over burger completely enclosing. Bake at 400 about 35 - 45 minutes. Remove, serve. Variation - wrap thin sliced bacon around each meat/cheese ball, secure with toothpick and deep fry. *Fun dinner or another party or game day favorite.*

Bacon Cheeseburger Puffs

4 oz bacon, slightly cooked, coarsely crumbled
1/2 pound ground beef
1 cup biscuit/baking mix
2 cups shredded Cheddar cheese
6-7 Tbps buttermilk

In a skillet, cook and crumble ground beef until no longer pink, drain. In a bowl, combine biscuit mix, bacon, and cheese; stir in cooked beef. Add buttermilk and toss with a fork until moistened.

Shape into 1-1/2-in. balls. Place 2 inches apart on ungreased baking sheet, or use muffin pan.

Preheat oven to 400 degrees. Bake for 12-15 minutes or until puffed and golden brown. Cool on wire racks. Remove and serve. Serves two.

Bacon Cherry Tomatoes

Cut each strip of bacon in thirds lengthwise. Wrap each bacon piece around a cherry tomato and thread them onto skewers. Grill indirectly over a medium fire until browned and crisp, about 10 minutes.

Bacon Chocolate Chip Pecan Cookies

5 strips bacon, cooked and finely chopped
1 cup all-purpose flour
1/2 teaspoon baking soda
1/2 teaspoon salt
1 stick (1/2 cup) unsalted butter at room temperature
1/2 cup white sugar
1/3 cup light brown sugar
1 large egg
1 teaspoon vanilla extract
2/3 cups semisweet chocolate chips
1/2 cup chopped pecans

Preheat oven to 350 degrees. Line two large baking sheets with parchment paper. In a medium bowl, whisk flour, baking soda, and salt. In a large bowl, cream butter and sugars, add egg and vanilla extract, and beat until blended. Add dry ingredients and beat until incorporated and the flour is dissolved. Stir in chocolate chips, pecans, and bacon.

Drop one large tablespoon cookie dough 2 to 3 inches apart on baking sheet. Bake for 10 to 12 minutes, or until golden brown around the edges, and slightly soft in the center. Transfer to a rack and cool for 15 minutes. Remove, eat.

Makes about 18 cookies. *Can be stored on countertop for one to two days if they last that long.*

Bacon Chipotle BBQ Sauce

from Culinaryginger.com

4 slices bacon, cooked, finely chopped (save the grease)
½ medium onion, finely chopped
2 cloves garlic, minced or grated
1 chipotle pepper with sauce, chopped - (La Morena chipotle peppers in adobo sauce)
2 tablespoons La Morena pickled jalapeno peppers, chopped
1 - 15 ounce can tomato sauce
2 tablespoons honey
1 tablespoon apple cider vinegar
1 tablespoon vegetable oil
Salt and ground pepper to taste

Add chopped onions to bacon grease and cook on medium until softened. add garlic and cook for one more minute, add chopped chipotle pepper, adobo sauce, jalapeños, tomato sauce, apple cider vinegar, vegetable oil, and honey, salt and pepper, stir well. Simmer for 10 minutes until thickened.

Allow the sauce to cool for 5 minutes, then transfer to a food processor or blender, and blend until smooth. Transfer to sterilized jars with lids and refrigerate for up to 2 weeks.

Bacon, Chocolate Covered

Melt half a cup of semi-sweet chocolate chips and quickly stir in a tablespoon of butter. This is a thick ganache that will be nice and shiny when set. Cover half slices bacon cooked rigid with a coat of the chocolate, (leave about inch at end uncoated for picking up to eat) lay flat on wax paper lined platter add three grains course sea salt to each piece and refrigerate. *OMG salty, sweet, bacon, chocolate, Yum!*

Bacon Chocolate Peanut Bark

8 strips bacon, thick sliced, cooked and crumbled
16 ounces semisweet chocolate
1 cup unsalted peanuts

Add chocolate to a double boiler. If you don't have one, fill a pan with a couple of inches of water. Place a glass bowl over the pan, making sure the bottom of the bowl does not touch the water underneath. Once the water begins to boil, add the chocolate. Using a spatula, stir continuously, until smooth and creamy.

Stir in bacon and peanuts. Pour onto a large baking sheet lined with parchment paper and spread to 3/8-inch thickness.

Refrigerate for a minimum of 1 hour. The bark should be hard and chilled. Cut into pieces and serve at room temperature.

Bacon Crème Brûlée

Eric and Julie Ireland have been serving up crème brûlée in Phoenix, Arizona, out of a big green food truck called Torched Goodness. One constant crowd pleaser is the Bacon Maple Crème Brûlée.

Bacon Croutons

Cut slab bacon in quarter inch chunks, cook as usual and enjoy. Much more bacon flavor in each bite. The French call these lardons. *Pop 'em like a snack and get your lardon.*

Bacon Cornflake Cookies

1/2 pound bacon, cooked and chopped
1/2 cup butter
3/4 cup sugar
1 egg
1 cup of flour
1/4 teaspoon baking soda
2 cups of multi-grain flakes or corn flakes
1/2 cup raisins

Preheat oven to 350 degrees. Beat together butter and sugar until fluffy, beat in egg. Combine flour and baking soda, stir into butter mixture, stir in bacon, flakes, and raisins.

Drop by rounded teaspoonfuls onto ungreased cookie sheet. Space two inches apart. Bake 15-18 minutes. Remove and eat.

Bacon Corn on the Cob

You are in for a real treat if you grill corn on the cob, then spread on bacon butter, instead of regular butter, then add salt. Or wrap each with a strip of thin sliced bacon and grill on unheated side of grill. *Yum!*

Bacon Deep Fried Doritos

Fry about ten slices of thick cut bacon, dredge in flour, brush with egg wash, then sprinkle crushed Doritos on top of each slice. Drop in deep fryer for about 30 seconds.

Bacon Easter Surprise

2 strips of bacon, cooked, cut into 2 inch slices
1 hollow chocolate bunny

Heat knife by running the blade under very hot water and dry. Cut bottom off of chocolate bunny and set bottom piece aside. Insert bacon pieces into the hollow bunny. Replace bottom piece on bunny and use warm knife to reseal.

Bacon Elvis

Wisconsin paid tribute to Elvis' famous sandwich with its on-a-stick creation, the Fat Elvis: a peanut butter cup dunked in banana batter, then deep-fried, and served with bacon on top.

Bacon Garlic Pumpkin Seeds

1 Tbsp bacon olive oil or bacon grease
1 1/2 tbsp bacon salt
pumpkin seeds from 1 medium pumpkin
1/2 tsp garlic powder

Preheat oven to 250 degrees F. In a bowl, mix pumpkin seeds with approximately 3-4 tbsp of melted bacon grease (depending on how many seeds you are making), mix in any flavor bacon salt and garlic powder.

Spread the pumpkin seeds evenly on a greased cookie sheet. Cook in oven for approximately 25-30 minutes, checking every 10 minutes for doneness.

Bacon Goat Cheese Stuffed Apples

6 pieces bacon, slightly cooked and crumbled
4 apples, cored
12 ounces soft goat cheese
1 tablespoon light cream
1 tablespoon butter
3 cloves garlic, minced
Salt and pepper to taste

Preheat oven to 375 degrees F. Lightly grease baking dish and place apples upright. Heat butter in a large skillet over medium high heat. Add garlic and cook until soft. Add cream and cook until liquid has mostly evaporated, about two minutes. Turn off heat and stir in goat cheese.

Scoop cheese mixture evenly into each apple, top with crumbled bacon, add salt and pepper to taste. Bake apples about 25 - 30 minutes, or until soft and cheese is bubbly. Remove, eat.

Bacon Hot Dog Bun

Create a bacon weave and place a hot dog wrapped in foil on top of it. Using more foil, wrap weave tightly around dog and freeze with dog side down for 10 minutes to keep it firm before cooking. Remove foil and cook with hot dog side down on cool side of grill until bacon is almost done. Remove dog and continue to grill bun with open side up until bacon is done. Remove, eat. (Note - Hamburger buns are easier, make 2 bacon weaves hamburger size, cook and use as bun.)

Bacon Hot Fudge Sundae

Put extra thick, crisp bacon strip halves on your hot fudge sundae.

Bacon Jerky

Bacon Jerky is pork strips that should be actual bacon, salted, smoked, and dried to preserve for later consumption.

During preparation, bacon should be dried quickly in order to limit bacterial growth on the still-moist meat: it is thinly sliced and then dried at low temperatures in order to avoid cooking or over-drying, which would result in a brittle product.

Unlike other forms of jerky, exotic marinades are not used to maintain the bacony flavor of the product.

Bacon Maple Citrus

Four 3/4-inch-thick slices of skinless slab bacon, cut in half
1/4 cup pure maple syrup
2 tablespoons sherry vinegar
1 teaspoon finely grated orange zest
1 teaspoon finely grated lime zest
Freshly snipped chives, for garnish

Preheat a grill pan or preheat oven to 375 F. In a small bowl, whisk the maple syrup with the vinegar and orange and lime zests. Grill the bacon over moderately low heat, turning occasionally, until lightly browned and tender, about 12 minutes. Brush with the maple-citrus syrup and continue grilling or cooking, turning occasionally, until glazed, 2 to 3 minutes longer. Remove, garnish with snipped chives, serve.

Bacon n Nuts

12 ounces thick cut bacon, slightly cooked and chopped into lardons
4 cups assorted nuts
1/2 teaspoon ground cumin
1/4 teaspoon cayenne pepper
1 large pinch ground nutmeg
1 large pinch of salt
2 tsp unsalted butter
1 tsp salt

Reserve the bacon fat drippings. Toast the nuts in a large, heavy based dry pan until golden, add the bacon fat drippings and butter to nuts and cook until the nuts begin to darken. Add a few drops of water and the bacon lardons and toss together. Put them in the oven for another five minutes at 160C to dry out. Remove, eat, or store in an airtight container.

Bacon Mashed Potato Cheese Balls

1 pound bacon
2 potatoes, diced and boiled
2 tablespoons butter
1 cup of dry breadcrumbs
1/2 cup milk
Oil for frying
Cheddar cheese cut into 1 inch cubes
Serves about 8

Dice two potatoes and boil them for about10 minutes. Mash potatoes and add milk plus butter and mix. Heat vegetable oil in a saucepan or small pot to approximately 350°F, Pour out 1 cup of dry breadcrumbs into a small bowl, take a portion of mashed potato mixture and form it around a cheddar cheese cube, roll it into bowl of dry breadcrumbs. Wrap each with one slice of bacon. Deep fry in oil for about 3-4 minutes. Drain, let cool, and serve.

Bacon Mushroom Caps

Fill mushroom caps with cheese and wrap with bacon for quick party snacks. Deep fry or bake - heat and eat.

Bacon Oatmeal Raisin Cookies

from bonappetit.com

6 slices bacon, cooked, chopped into 1/4 inch bits
1 rounded cup
1/2 teaspoon baking powder
1/2 teaspoon kosher salt
1/2 teaspoon baking soda
1/2 cup (packed) dark brown sugar
1/3 cup sugar
1/4 cup unsalted butter, room temperature
1 large egg
1/4 teaspoon vanilla extract
1/2 cup old-fashioned oats
2/3 cup raisins

Line 2 baking sheets with parchment paper. Whisk flour, baking powder, salt, and baking soda in a medium bowl. Beat both sugars and butter in a large bowl, mix in egg and vanilla, mix in dry ingredients. Fold bacon, oats, and raisins into batter until evenly incorporated. Form dough into 9 even size balls, place evenly spaced on sheets. Cover and chill dough for 1 hour overnight.

Preheat to 375° F., bake cookies, after 10 minutes, rotate pans, continue cooking another 10 minutes or until edges are light golden brown and centers are still soft. Let cool on baking sheets for 10 minutes. Transfer to a wire rack to cool more. Remove, serve.

Bacon Oreo Glazed

Remove the filling from one package of Oreo cookies. Put all the filling in a bowl and microwave it for 60 seconds to melt. Stir.

Take a pastry brush and brush the melted Oreo filling onto one side of thick sliced bacon, slightly cooked and sliced in half. Place bacon in 350° oven for five minutes, flip, brush other side of each slice with melted filling and bake for another five minutes. Remove, sprinkle crushed Oreos on each slice, cool, serve.

Bacon Oreos

St. Louis cocktail bar Taste has the Pigwich, a homemade bacon Oreo. The pastry chef was making Oreo-like cookies, but using a pig cookie cutter and decided it needed real pig meat. The slightly salty, malted milk chocolate cookies paired perfectly with smoked pork fat frosting.

Bacon Parmesan Pretzels

10 slices of thin cut bacon
10 pretzel rods
1 cup parmesan cheese
garlic powder to taste

Wrap spiral slice of bacon around each pretzel rod, leaving one inch unwrapped at one end. Place on a microwave safe dish covered with two layers of paper towels. Microwave for 2 to 2.5 minutes or until bacon is cooked to a golden brown. Remove and roll each pretzel rod in a plate covered with parmesan cheese and garlic powder mix. Stand upright in a mug or attractive dish to serve.

Bacon Pinwheels

6 slices bacon, cooked and crumbled
1 can crescent roll dough
4 eggs, scrambled
1 cup cheddar cheese, shredded
paprika or cayenne pepper to taste

Preheat oven to 350° F. Unroll crescent roll dough and split it up into two rectangles that are each 12″ x 4″.

Spread toppings evenly over the dough and roll up each rectangle. Slice each roll of dough into six pinwheels. Easier to cut if chilled.

Place the pinwheels on a cookie sheet and cook for 15 minutes or until the crescent roll dough is a golden brown. Remove, serve.

Bacon Pizza Balls

1-2 pounds thick cut bacon, lightly cooked, sliced in 4 pieces each
3 (10-count) packages buttermilk biscuits
block of cheddar or your choice cheese
1 egg, beaten
Parmesan cheese grated
Italian seasoning
garlic powder
1 jar pizza sauce

Slice cheese into approximately 30 small squares, flatten each biscuit and stack bacon and cheese on top. Gather edges of biscuit and pinch to secure on top. Line rolls in greased 9x13 baking pan.

Brush with beaten egg. Sprinkle with Parmesan cheese, Italian seasoning, and garlic powder. Bake at 425 degrees for 18 to 20 minutes. Remove and serve with warm pizza sauce for dipping.

Bacon Poutine

Poutine with hand-cut fries, scratch gravy, fresh white cheddar curds, and hand-chopped bacon. *Bacon makes everything taste better.*

Bacon Pumpkin Pie

Add seven pieces of cooked crumbled bacon into the pumpkin mixture before baking, then add more crumbles on top after it comes out of the oven. An alternative filling is Rhubarb, one of my favorites.

Bacon Popcorn

Place 16 slices bacon on a rack in a baking pan, top with 1/2 cup brown sugar and bake at 400 degrees until crisp, 12 minutes, then chop.

Make stove-popped corn using bacon drippings in place of oil. Toss the popcorn with the sweet luscious bacon, salt. Variation - also sprinkle grated parmesan over cooked bacon popcorn. Tastes better than theater cheese flavor.

Bacon Popcorn Cheddar

Trader Joe's sells Baconesque White Cheddar Popcorn. *Actually, quite good and reasonably priced.*

Bacon Potato Parmesan Bread

1 cup cooked, finely chopped bacon
3 tablespoons olive oil, divided
2 cups flour
1 Tablespoon baking powder
1/2 teaspoon salt
3/4 cup chilled mashed potatoes
3/4 cup Shredded Parmesan Cheese
1 large egg
milk as needed

Preheat oven to 375 degrees. Butter a pie pan. Sift flour, baking powder and salt into a bowl. Mix bacon, cheese, and mashed potatoes thoroughly into mixture.

Pour olive oil into a measuring cup, and beat in egg. Add enough milk to make 3/4 cup and mix well.

Fold wet mixture into dry mixture, but do not overwork. Put dough on a floured surface and gently knead. Pat dough into the bottom of pie pan.

Bake until toothpick inserted in center comes out clean, 35- 40 minutes. Remove, cool, and serve at room temperature.

Bacon Potato Chips

5 - 7 slices thin cut bacon
2 large russet potatoes
Oil for frying
Salt to taste

Clean and dry potatoes, then using a mandolin or sharp knife, make long even lengthwise slices. Make them thick enough so the potato does not tear when inserting the bacon. You should get about 10-15 chips each.

Make two cuts in center of the potato about one half inch apart and just wide enough to hold the bacon. Cut bacon to match length of potatoes then lightly cook.

In a separate pan, heat up oil to cover potato slices, on medium heat. Fry each potato slice for 10 - 15 seconds each then drain. Let cool enough to handle, then insert the partially cooked bacon piece into the center cuts.

Heat oil to 350 degrees and fry, or broil until potatoes golden and bacon cooked. Remove, eat.

Bacon Pretzels

1 pound thin cut bacon, cut in half
1 package pretzel rods, cut in half
2 cups brown sugar
dash cayenne pepper
package or two unsweetened chocolate
course sea salt to taste

Mix brown sugar and cayenne in a medium size bowl and then spread it out on a large flat dish.

Coat each strip of bacon on both sides with the brown sugar mixture. Pressing firmly to adhere. Spiral wrap bacon around the pretzel, leaving end exposed to pick up with fingers after cooked.

Warm chocolate in top of double boiler until soft enough for dipping.

Place on wire rack on top of a baking sheet. Keep tail end of bacon under pretzel to avoid unwrap.

Bake at 375 F for about 10 minutes or until bacon is fully cooked. Remove, dip in melted chocolate, very lightly sprinkle sea salt while chocolate still warm, let cool on cookie rack. Remove, serve.

Bacon Faux Pretzels

Fold two strips of thick sliced bacon in half lengthwise. Twist together and secure with at toothpick at each end or use long (wet so it does not burn) skewer to hold shape. Make many as these will go fast. Bake on wire rack above foil lined cookie pan at 375 f until done. Remove and eat. Fun when served with dipping cheese or chocolate.

Bacon Rice Krispies

4 strips of thick sliced bacon, cooked and chopped
3 Tablespoons butter
1 ten ounce package regular marshmallows or 4 cups miniature
6 cups Rice Krispies®

Melt butter in saucepan, add marshmallows and stir until melted, add Rice Krispies and stir until evenly coated, add chopped bacon and stir until evenly mixed. Coat a 13 x 9 x 2 inch pan with cooking spray or line with wax paper or sprayed foil, add mixture to pan, smooth to even height, let cool. Remove, cut into squares, serve.

Bacon Ritz Crackers

The Nabisco cracker company released its new bacon-flavored Ritz Crackers with black pepper seasoning.

Bacon Scallops

4 ounces thin sliced bacon, cut in half
1 large grapefruit

1.25 lb. sea scallops
1/4 cup onion
1/2 cup sauvignon blanc
2 Tbsp. capers
2 Tbsp. unsalted butter
salt to taste
Ground pepper

Peel grapefruit, removing all of the bitter white pith. Cut in between the membranes to release the sections. Squeeze juice from the membrane into another bowl; you should have about 3 tablespoons of juice.

Cook bacon until crisp, remove, save 1 tablespoon of the bacon fat.

Season scallops with salt and pepper, add to the skilletalong with the bacon fat, and cook over moderate high heat until browned, 3 minutes. Turn, add onion, and cook over moderate heat until the scallops are just cooked through, 3 minutes longer. Transfer to a plate.

Add wine and grapefruit juice to the same skillet and bring to a simmer over moderate heat. Cook, scraping up any browned bits. Strain the liquid into a heatproof cup, then return it to the skillet. Add the capers and butter, cook until the sauce is thickened, 2 to 3 minutes. Add back the scallops and any juices to the skillet, turn to coat them with the sauce. Remove, add grapefruit sections, bacon and serve.

Bacon Shoestrings

Julienne very cold slab bacon to make shoestrings, spread in thin layer on foil lined cooking sheet, broil, remove, eat. Variation, when half done sprinkle with parmesan cheese, finish cooking. remove and serve warm or cold.

Bacon S'Mores

Cook thick sliced bacon cut in half, until stiff, then spread melted marshmallows over each stiff bacon strip. Sprinkle crushed graham crackers on the marshmallows. Put in oven for two minutes at 400° F. Melt semi sweet chocolate for dipping. Tip - keep wide mouth jar with chocolate in crock pot set on low, with water to half up side of jar. Will keep chocolate ready for dipping all day.

Bacon S'Mores Maple

Cook maple bacon, let cool and chop. Add bacon to melted chocolate, and spread on graham crackers. Roast marshmallows over open flame and press on top.

Bacon Spam

Spam is flavored with bacon, happiness is everywhere, but mostly in the frying pan. It is about time these two meat candy porcine compatriots got together.

Bacon Spicy

1 pound thick-cut bacon
1/2 cup flour
1/2 cup brown sugar
2 t cayenne pepper

Preheat oven to 400 and line a large baking sheet with tinfoil. Combine flour, sugar, and cayenne in a large zip-lock bag or large flat plate. Coat bacon with mixture by tossing a few slices at a time into the bag or press into plated mixture. Lay out bacon slices on baking sheet and cook for 15-25 minutes, after 15 minutes, watch carefully. Remove and serve, or can be reheated.

Bacon Sriracha Jerky

Trader Joe's sells Sweet Sriracha Uncured Bacon Jerky. It is a bit more hot than sweet, but some folks like it that way.

Bacon Stuffed Pears

Stuff pear halves with Ricotta or cottage cheese, chopped walnuts, chopped bacon, and honey. Warm in oven and serve warm.

Bacon Tater Tots

1 pound thin sliced bacon, each strip cut into 4 pieces
1 bag tater tots

2/3 cup brown sugar
1 teaspoon chili powder

Preheat oven to 375 degrees. Line a cookie sheet with foil and place a cooling rack on top of the pan. In a small bowl, mix brown sugar and chili powder until well combined.

Wrap each thawed tater tot in bacon and then roll it in the mixture. Secure bacon for cooking with toothpick. Place on top of the cooling rack and bake about 10 to 15 minutes at 375 F, then increase heat to 400 F for another 5 minutes. Remove and serve warm. Can also sprinkle grated cheese over all while still hot.

Bacon Tempura

12 strips thick sliced bacon, slightly cooked
canola oil
2 egg whites
1 1/2 cups flour
1 1/2 cups club soda
salt to taste

Pour oil into a heavy medium pot or a wok to a depth of 2" and heat over medium heat until temperature registers 375° on a candy thermometer.

Whisk egg whites in a large bowl until soft peaks form. Using a rubber spatula, fold one-quarter of the flour, one-quarter of club soda at a time into whites, folding thoroughly after each addition until batter is smooth. Place batter in refrigerator to cool.

Working in batches, dip bacon into cool batter, then deep-fry, turning once, until bacon is golden brown and crisp, about 6 minutes per batch. Drain on a wire rack. Remove, salt and serve warm. Serves four.

Bacon Weave Ice Cream Sandwich

Create two square bacon weaves from thin sliced bacon, cut weaves depending on ice cream package shape, cook in oven until crispy. Eat leftover pieces while slicing a pint of ice cream into 3/4 inch thick slabs. Place between bacon weaves and enjoy.

Bacon Wrapped Bacon

Get slab bacon, cut into half inch squares, cook until half done, let cool and wrap with thin sliced bacon cut in half, put in oven and cook until done. Serve hot or cold. For dipping use toothpicks and set out small bowls of warm chocolate, or melted cheese, or strawberry jelly, or peanut butter. *Be brave use all four.*

Bacon Wrapped Crackers

1 pound thin sliced bacon (or more), slightly cooked, cut in half
1 package club crackers
grated parmesan cheese or brown sugar

Lay crackers face up on a cookie sheet, scoop about one teaspoon of cheese onto each cracker. Cut bacon in half, spoon generous portion of cheese or brown sugar on each, wrap each covered cracker in one half piece of bacon in one direction and another slice in perpendicular direction covering the cracker and wrapped under. Place bacon wrapped crackers ontofoil lined baking sheet with a rack on it, put in a 300-degree oven for about an hour. Check frequently after 45 minutes. Remove, serve.

Bacon Wrapped Cherries

2 packages thin sliced bacon, cut in half
about 32 pitted cherries
1/4 cup honey
1 Tbsp brown sugar
1 tsp cinnamon
about 7 BBQ Skewers - soaked in water for 20 minutes before cooking, to keep from burning.

Mix honey, cinnamon, and brown sugar in small container and set aside.

Wrap each half-strip of bacon around each cherry. Place skewer in the end of the bacon strip, through the center of the cherry, and out the other side. Repeat until each skewer has 5 or 6 wrapped cherries.

Baste, place skewers on grill or under broiler and cook until partially done, flip cherries and baste again with the honey mixture. After basting, let cook for another few minutes. Remove and serve warm.

Bacon Wrapped Grilled Corn

Wrap corn with strips of bacon in a loose spiral, attach with toothpicks, grill, season to taste, eat, enjoy.

Bacon Wrapped Pizza

Put some mozzarella cheese in an ice cube tray, cover in pizza sauce, place in freezer. Take frozen ball of cheese and sauce and coat with flour, dip in egg wash and roll in panko breadcrumbs. Completely wrap each with thin sliced bacon and deep-fry for a few minutes. *Hats off to Dude Foods for this goodie.*

Bacon Wrapped Peanut Butter

Spoon peanut butter into an ice cube tray and put in freezer. After frozen, take out and roll in flour, then dip in egg wash, then roll in breadcrumbs, then wrap each with two slices of thin sliced maple bacon. *Hats off to Dude Foods for this goodie, also.*

Bacon Wrapped Smokies with Brown Sugar

1 pound thin sliced bacon cut into thirds
1 stick butter
1 pound little smokies
2 cups brown sugar

Preheat oven to 375F. Wrap each smokie and place all the wrapped smokies in a single layer on a baking dish. Melt butter, add 1 cup of brown sugar, and stir until mixed well. Pour butter and brown sugar mixture over smokies and bacon. Take the other cup of brown sugar and sprinkle evenly over the smokies. Bake for about 20 to 25 minutes and then turn the heat up to 400F for about 5 minutes or longer until the bacon becomes glazed and crispy. Can be put in crock pot and served warm all day.

Tale of Two Pigs

Two Irishmen, Paddy and Paddy went out one day and each bought a pig. When they got home, Paddy turned to Paddy and said, "Paddy, me ol' mate, how are we going to tell who owns which darn pig?" Paddy says, "Well Paddy, I'll cut one of te ears off me pig, and den we can tell them apart."

"Ah, dat id be grand," says Paddy.

This worked fine until a couple of weeks later, when Paddy stormed into the house. "Paddy" he said, "Your darn pig has chewed the ear off me darn pig. Now we got two pigs with one ear each. How are we going to tell who owns which darn pig?"

"Well Paddy," says Paddy, "I'll cut ta other ear off me darn pig. Den we'll ave two pigs and only one of them will av an ear."

"Ah tat'd be grand," says Paddy.

Again, this worked fine until a couple of weeks later, when Paddy again stormed into the house. "Paddy", he said, "Your darn pig has chewed the other ear offa me darn pig. Now, we got two pigs with no darn ears. How we gonna tell who owns which pig?"

"Ah, dis is serious, Paddy" said Paddy. "I'll tell ya what I'll do. I'll cut de tail offa my darn pig. Den we'll av two pigs with no darn ears and only one darn tail."

"Ah tat'd be grand," says Paddy.

Another couple of weeks went by and Paddy stormed into the house once more. "Paddy," shouted Paddy, "Your darn pig has chewed the darn tail offa me pig, and now we got two pigs with no darn ears and no darn tails. How de heck are we gonna tell 'em apart?"

"Ah, da heck with it" says Paddy, "How's about you have da black one, and I'll have da white one."

Did you know the mirrors on motorcycles are called pig spotters?

BACON DRINKS

High-end cocktail bars have begun serving their drinks with dense, extra-large cubes. Experts have found small ice tends to dilute drinks and reduce flavor.

For colder and less diluted drinks, such as those included here, use larger ice cubes, like the football shaped N'ice Balls from Douglas Trading Company   http://www.douglastradingcompany.com/

Bacon Apple Martini

4 oz. of bacon-infused Vodka
4 oz. Applejack
2 oz. Amaretto liqueur
2 oz. pure Maple syrup
2 oz. sparkling apple cider
2-4 slices candied bacon, cut in half (see recipe earlier in this book)

Pre-chill 4 martini glasses. In a large cocktail shaker, combine bacon-infused vodka, applejack, amaretto, sparkling apple cider and maple syrup with ice. Shake until mixture is ice-cold. Strain into the 4 chilled glasses and garnish each with 1-2 slices of candied bacon. Drink.

Bacon Baby Formula

How about something for that new child or grandchild. Here is just the thing, Bacon flavored formula. *Get them started early.*

Bacon Beer

Voodoo Doughnut Bacon Maple Ale
by Rogue Beers - *Wow!*

Bacon Bloody Mary Beast

Milwaukee bar, Sobelman's has a bacon topped Bloody Mary drink named "Chicken Fried Bloody Beast," that features cheese, sausage, pickles, olives, onions, mushrooms, asparagus, scallions, shrimp, lemon, Brussels sprouts, tomatoes, celery, bacon-wrapped jalapeno cheese balls, and an entire fried chicken.

Bacon Coffee

Starbucks subsidiary brand Seattle's Best have combed state fairs across the country and are officially gearing up to release a bacon coffee drink.

The new flavor combines Level 5 Seattle's Best Coffee, caramelized bacon, and subtle hints of pumpkin pie spice. It is a result of a country-wide search for the most "imaginative new coffee drink."

The winner was Des Moines native Eileen Fannon, who calls her concoction the "How to Win a Guy with One Sip." The key to America's collective male heart is apparently coffee with bacon. *Of course, we have known the key is bacon alone or with anything for centuries.*

The coffee drink will also be featured in participating Seattle's Best Coffee locations across North America.

Bacon Hangover Recipe

Although not a drink, hangovers come with drinking so I thought this is the perfect spot for a hangover recipe.

A study at the Newcastle University's Center for Life examined just why a bacon sandwich could be the perfect culinary treat to absorb all that alcohol. Researcher Elin Roberts says it is because of the mix of bread and the amino-acids found in bacon. She told the London Times, *"Bread doesn't soak up alcohol, but is high in carbohydrates that boost blood-sugar levels and speed up the metabolism, helping to get rid of alcohol quickly. Bingeing on alcohol depletes brain neurotransmitters, but bacon, which is rich in protein, contains amino acids that top these up and make you feel better."*

What is an open-face sandwich on thick Texas toast, with turkey, bacon, and rich cheesy Mornay sauce? It is a Hot Brown. The

Brown Hotel was a center of Louisville, Kentucky's social life in the 1920s, with dinner dances that would stretch far into the night. So its chef, Fred Schmidt, devised a meal that would sell like crazy. It is still on the menu at the Brown Hotel, and elsewhere in the region.

A proper Hot Brown starts with thick-cut Texas toast, crusts removed. That toast is layered with slices of fresh roast turkey, tomatoes, and a ladle of rich Mornay (a béchamel-based sauce with Pecorino Romano). After oven cooked, it is topped with thick-cut bacon. The Brown Hotel has one almost identical to the version invented back in the '20s.

Gary's, on Spring, offers a comparatively delicate Baby Hot Brown on its appetizer menu.

Bristol Bar & Grille inverts the normal order of the classic with a Hot Brown Soup, a cheesy soup base with ham and turkey, garnished with crostini, bacon, and chopped tomatoes.

Dish, on Market, has an eggs Benedict, with poached eggs joining the roast turkey, applewood-smoked bacon, and Texas toast, plus cheddar and tomato, all doused in Mornay.

Bacon Maple Caesar Cocktail

Mix Clamato juice, Worcestershire sauce, hot sauce, bacon infused vodka, fresh grated horseradish. Rim garnished with bacon salt and finished with a crunchy slice of maple bacon (one bite per sip).

Bacon Maple Coffee

From Firehouse Coffee - Bacon & Maple Syrup coffee has delicious flavors of sweet maple syrup and crispy Canadian bacon to brew an American breakfast taste. With initial hints of a bacon taste you will notice a smooth maple syrup that will cross the palate to cause a rapid combustion of your taste buds. Fidel Castro and Rush Limbaugh are both known to love this. CoffeeAM online also has Maple Bacon Coffee.

Bacon Maple Coffee Porter

Funky Buddha Brewery makes an award winning Maple Bacon Coffee Porter. It's rated as the number 3 porter in the world according to RateBeer.com. Nimble Hill Brewing also has Midnight Fuggle Bacon Maple Coffee Porter.

Maple Bacon Frappe

1/4 cup Torani bacon flavoring syrup
1 1/2 cups ice cubes
3/4 cup strong brew maple bacon coffee
1/2 cup milk
2 Tablespoons maple syrup
whipped cream

Brew coffee and let it cool. Add the ingredients into blender in the order listed above, except whipped cream. Blend all ingredients until frothy and smooth. Pour into desired glasses and top with whipped cream and a drizzle of maple syrup.

Bacon Shake

Jack in the Box has a Bacon Milkshake. The fast food chain felt the need to create some bacon buzz as part of a new ad campaign that asks: "If you like bacon so much, why don't you marry it?"

Jack's misstep is that is just a bacon flavored syrup added to a shake. Word from some is that the real taste is Ugh! *Oh, well, give them credit for trying to get on the bacon bandwagon. Too bad it doesn't pass the sniff test.*

Bacon Spice

One part spiced rum, one part bacon vodka, two parts ginger ale. Mix, enjoy. (Vernor's Ginger ale is especially good for this.)

Bakon Vodka

It costs about $30 a bottle. Can you think of a Bloody Mary with a hint of bacon? *Great for the day after or even the day before.*

A friend of mine, Joe Dougherty makes his own bacon infused vodka. Easy to do, but it takes patience, many steps, and many days to steep the bacon.

Bacon is the duct tape of kitchens.

BACON RECIPE ADDENDA

Adding Bacon to Recipes

- Hickory, apple-wood and maple-smoked bacon lend themselves especially well to sweet desserts.

- Keep the flavors simple and create a pleasing contrast of both flavor and texture. The idea is to make the familiar more exciting.

- Wraps usually do better with thin sliced bacon, so it cooks faster.

- Chopped bacon can be either thin or thick sliced.

- Hearty dishes with thick sliced bacon add more flavor.

- Make sure bacon is slightly cooked and dry when adding to other ingredients for further cooking.

- Bacon strips will keep your meatloaf from sticking to the pan while it cooks. Place a strip or two on the bottom of a cooking pan to stop meatloaf and other casseroles from sticking. Works great for flour or bread dishes to also make them less sticky.

Most bacon purists will never taint a sandwich or many recipes with anything that was at some point a green plant or attached in any way to a green plant. Some call them bacon vegans.

Bacon as a Snack

For those on high-protein, low-carbohydrate diets, bacon makes a great snack when fried up crispy. It supplies a crunch that is often missed on these diets, while most of the fat is rendered out. A standard cooked slice of bacon contains about 30 to 40 calories per slice, and less if you cook it slowly until crisp and drain well.

Bacon and Baseball

The **Texas Rangers** have many bacon items at Globe Life Park beginning in the 2015 season, including bacon beer, bacon cotton candy, bacon sunflower seeds, candied bacon with cinnamon and chili powder, bacon lollipops, bacon sunflower seeds, and chicken fried bacon on a stick. The bacon beer comes from Oregon-based Rogue Breweries.

The **West Michigan Whitecaps** minor league baseball club is running a contest to determine what new food item will be available at the Fifth Third Ballpark, where they play home games this season.

One of the items is Chocolate Covered Bacon – *This little piggy went to market, this little piggy stayed home and this little piggy dunked itself in chocolate to become a delicious treat.*

Bacon Cups

2 pounds thin sliced bacon, cut bacon in thirds or quarters to fit pan size.

Preheat oven to 350 degrees F. Turn a mini muffin pan upside-down and coat the bottom with nonstick pan spray. Crisscross 3 slices of bacon over each upturned cup, and then place another sprayed mini muffin pan on top so that the bacon slices are compressed between the two pans. Place the pans on a rimmed baking sheet and bake until the bacon cups are crisp and browned, about 25 minutes.

Remove from oven and set aside to cool. Lift off the top pan. Remove the bacon cups from the bottom pan and place them on a paper-towel-lined baking sheet to drain, bottom up.

If you want to waste a few bucks you can also buy things made specifically to create bacon cups in the microwave. It is called the (As seen on TV) 'perfect bacon bowl'. Two for a dollar at Dollar Tree.

Bacon de Provence

This is bacon with an unusual flavoring, herbs de Provence. These subtly smoked strips are fringed with mixtures typically marjoram, rosemary, thyme, and oregano.

Bacon Dust Tater Tots

Tater Tots with Pork Remoulade and Bacon Dust; from Chambers Eat and Drink, San Francisco. While the tots sell the dish, the killer component is a spicy, tangy sauce that is kicked up a notch by rendered bacon bits and pork scraps. He mixes bacon fat, salt and tapioca maltodextrin (a fat stabilizer) together, passes it through a sieve and creates a powder that is bacon addictive.

Bacon Grill

This is a canned meat product, but in Ireland and United Kingdom is made fresh and made from chopped and cured pork (and sometimes chicken), seasoned to be similar in flavor to bacon. Manufactured in the Netherlands, it is produced by Princes for the British market, in the style of Spam and corned beef. Bacon Grill was a standard element of rations in the British Army.

Ingredients of Bacon Grill seem to vary; a can of 'Celebrity Bacon Grill lists: pork (64%), water, starch, pork fat, pork rind, salt, milk protein, stabilizer (Sodium Triphosphorate), smoke flavor, sugar, preservative (Sodium Nitrite), spice extracts.

Prince's Bacon Grill lists: Pork (43%), mechanically recovered chicken (16%), water, wheat starch, pork fat, pork rind, salt, sodium caseinate, stabilizers, smoke flavoring, pepper extract, antioxidant, preservative.

Plumrose Bacon Grill lists: Pork (43%), mechanically recovered pork, water, pork fat, maize starch, pork rind, salt, milk protein, stabilizer (sodium triphosphate), smoke flavor, sugar, preservative (sodium nitrite), spice extracts.

Samgyeopsal

This is a popular Korean dish commonly served as an evening meal, it consists of thick, fatty slices of pork belly meat (similar to uncured bacon). The meat, usually neither marinated nor seasoned, is cooked on a grill at the diners' table. Usually diners grill the meat themselves and eat directly from the grill. It is often dipped into a spicy pepper paste.

Bacon Marinade

Make a paste of coffee grounds, brown sugar, and pinch of cayenne and let bacon sleep in it for a few hours. The coffee gives the bacon an added depth - *as if it needs more depth, but sometimes it is fun to change things a bit.*

Bacon Sandwiches

A **Fool's Gold Loaf,** mostly in Colorado, US consists of a single warmed, hollowed-out loaf of bread filled with one jar of creamy peanut butter, one jar of grape jelly, and a pound of bacon.

Hot Brown in Louisville, Kentucky, US open-faced with turkey and bacon, topped with Mornay sauce, and baked or broiled.

Bacon Gerber in Saint Louis, Missouri, US half section of Italian or French bread with garlic butter, containing ham, bacon, provolone cheese, topped with paprika, then toasted.

Bacon sandwiches are an all-day favorite throughout the United Kingdom. They are often served in greasy spoons, and are often recommended as a hangover cure.

Australian hamburger shops sell a bacon sandwich, which is made much like a traditional Australian hamburger with fried bacon, fried onions, lettuce, tomato, tinned beetroot and barbecue sauce or tomato sauce. In some places the sandwich is made from bread toasted on only one side. Some places serve it on hamburger buns.

In Toronto, Canada, peameal bacon (rolled cured and trimmed boneless loin in dried and ground yellow peas) is served on a Kaiser roll.

Irish formula - Place at least three carefully chosen bacon rashers on grill pan. Insert grill pan under grill (broiler). Cook until sizzling, then turn over the rashers, and cook other side until sizzling. In the meantime, cut two hunks of Kelly's small loaf. Butter liberally with real butter. According to taste, apply your favorite sauce to the bread. Evenly spread the hot rashers on the bread, top, and eat.

Perfect Bacon Sandwich

Experts at Leeds University discovered the secret to the ideal sandwich, after four researchers at the Department of Food Science spent more than 1,000 hours testing 700 variations of a traditional bacon sandwich.

They tried different types and cuts of bacon, cooking techniques, types of oil and a range of cooking times at different temperatures. They found that two or three back bacon rashers (slices) should be cooked under a preheated oven grill (broiler) for seven minutes at about 240C (475F).

The bacon should then be placed between two slices of farmhouse bread, 1cm to 2cm (1/2-3/4 inch) thick. They concluded that is not only the taste and smell of bacon that consumers find most attractive, but that texture and how crispy and crunchy rashers are. *Side note - A rasher of bacon can also be used to mean a 'portion' or 'serving' of bacon, not just a single slice. Also, streaky bacon is the British term for American style bacon.*

Bacon Waffling

According to some people, waffle irons or George Foreman type grills make the best bacon. In a pan, the fat and meat shrink and cook at different rates. The waffle iron pulls away bacon grease in its nooks and notches and the grills let run off to a catcher. You can easily pour off or leave a thin layer of bacony goodness on the waffle iron for extra good home-style waffles.

Bacon Weaves

There are many uses for bacon weaves. You can cook up a batch of bacon weaves and save in refrigerator for future use. Here are a few twists to the favorite hand food to try at home.

Use bacon weaves:

- As wraps for any kind of veggies,
- In place of bread for super grilled cheese or fried bologna and cheese,
- In place of bread for ultimate BLT,
- In place of bread for peanut butter and jelly sandwiches (peanut butter both sides, jelly in middle (add sliced banana for Elvis style),
- In place of dough for pizza,
- In place of bun for hot dogs, burgers, or sausage,
- In place of bun for egg McMuffins,
- In place of bun for superb barbecue pulled pork,
- In place of shell for perfect tacos.

World's Most Expensive Bacon Sandwich

The Bacon Bling sandwich, named by the World Record Academy as the world's most expensive bacon sandwich, costs $237 (£150). It can be found at the Tangberry coffee house in Cheltenham, Gloucestershire and contains an impressive list of ingredients. Some of the ingredients included are 7 rashers of rare breed pig bacon, sliced truffles, saffron, a free range egg, and edible gold dust.

Currently Guinness World Records does not consider this sandwich to be considered a record setter, but owner Paul Philips is hoping to change this by establishing a new category devoted to the world's most expensive commercially available bacon butty. The money you spend will be donated to charity, which is the reason behind the sandwich initiation.

Chicken Fried Bacon Creator

The creator of chicken fried bacon, Frank Sodolak has passed away. Thirty years ago Frank Sodolak borrowed a few hundred dollars and made his idea a reality in a small restaurant Sodolak's Original Country Inn in Snook Texas, population about 500. It is about 80 miles from Houston. His bacon delight has been featured in Maxim Magazine, Discovery Channel, Travel Channel and more.

If a pig is disgruntled, does that mean it has laryngitis?

Hamlet is a play, not a little pig.

A warthog does not come from crossing a pig and a frog.

Bacon Recipes on the Web

When you finish testing all of the recipes in this book, the following links, in no particular order, are a few web sites for more bacon recipe goodness:

http://bacontoday.com/junk-food-bacon-recipes/

http://bacon.wikia.com/wiki/Category:Bacon_Recipes

http://www.kitchendaily.com/read/15-mind-blowing-bacon-dishes#show-gallery

http://www.foodnetwork.com/recipes/articles/50-things-to-make-with-bacon.html

http://culinaryarts.about.com/lr/bacon_recipes/305610/1/

http://www.thedailymeal.com/15-mind-blowing-bacon-dishes

http://www.endlesssimmer.com/2009/08/18/100-ways-to-use-a-stick-of-bacon/

http://baconbaconbacon.tumblr.com/archive

http://www.endlesssimmer.com/featured/endless-bacon/

Many bacon bits sold at the supermarkets are actually vegetarian and unworthy of the name.

Bacon Drippings

THE RULES OF
BACON

1. THERE MUST ALWAYS BE BACON IN THE FRIDGE. ALWAYS.
2. THERE DOES NOT EXIST A FOOD THAT DOES NOT GO WELL WITH BACON.
3. THERE ARE TWO KINDS OF PEOPLE IN THE WORLD: THOSE WHO LIKE BACON, AND THOSE WHO WILL BE USED AS FODDER IN THE CASE OF A ZOMBIE APOCALYPSE.
4. EVEN PIGS LIKE BACON. FACT.
5. CRISPY AND CHEWY ARE BOTH ACCEPTABLE WAYS TO COOK BACON. THOU SHALT NOT DISCRIMINATE.
6. 90% OF THE WORLD'S PROBLEMS CAN BE SOLVED BY COOKING MORE BACON.
7. BACON PRESENTS EXACTLY ZERO HEALTH RISKS. SHUT UP.
8. IF YOUR COMPUTER IS ANTIQUATED AND SLOW, YOU CAN FEED IT BACON THROUGH THE FLOPPY DRIVE TO MAKE IT RUN FASTER.
9. MEALS WITHOUT BACON ARE RARELY WORTH EATING.
10. WHEN GIVEN A BREATHALYZER, THE NUMBER THEY GIVE YOU IS YOUR BAC. THIS IS SHORT FOR "BACON," AND IS EQUAL TO THE NUMBER OF SLICES OF BACON YOU SHOULD EAT DIVIDED BY 100.
11. THOU SHALT ALWAYS CONSUME BACON ON THE SABBATH. AND THE MONDATH. AND THE TUESDATH. AND THE....
12. BACON GETS YOU LAID.

2010-2011 SOMETHINGOFTHATILK.COM

Love is not difficult for a man to say if the next word is bacon.

BACON ITEMS

No one can possibly inventory all of the bacon items available for sale or as collectibles. There are stores dedicated to all bacon items, web sites dedicated to all bacon items. I have tried to pull a goodly number of interesting things together for your reading pleasure.

There are bacon summer camps, bacon film festivals, bacon bars, baconnaise, bacon lip balm, bacon soda, bacon air fresheners, bacon lube, bacon shaving cream, bacon deodorant and more.

Bacon may be finally closing in on importance to make a sale with the most important word in advertising - 'free'.

Bacon Quotient

The bacon quotient is that point at which a person can eat no more bacon (during any given sitting). For some it is as low as a half dozen strips and to another it might be four or more pounds. It is possible to increase a person's bacon quotient by eating more bacon.

Bacon Air Freshener

It smells like, well, you know, cooking bacon. For those times when you don't have time to cook up a batch. It costs only $2.95 on the web. *Aren't you glad I shared this one.*

Bacon Alarm Clock

My favorite - It is called 'Wake n Bacon' - an alarm clock that wakes you up with the smell and sizzle of cooking bacon, because no one likes to wake to an alarm. This clock gently wakes you up with the mouthwatering aroma of fresh cooked bacon. *Makes me want to take a nap, just to wake up.*

Bacon Air

You can actually suck bacon-flavored air out of an oxygen inhaler. That way, you get the life-sustaining goodness of bacon, along with your oxygen.

Bacon Balm

Sneak a rub in the summer and slather your lips in this bacon balm.

Bacon Bandages

A friend of mine, Jeff Flanagan came back from a recent trip and gave me a gift of bacon bandages he picked up along the way. (Likely after a few IPAs) Anyway, the gift was a tin of real bandages.

I quickly went home to administer a small cut on my hand to test the 'die cut sterile strips' and see how they worked. It really is a good mini bacon replica. Alas, it does not have the bacony goodness smell, but it is a true bandage. However, it also makes me hungry just looking at it. Time for breakfast. *Thanks Jeff.*

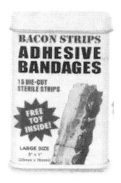

Bacon Board Game

"Mr. Bacon's Big Adventure," players can navigate through the Mustard Marsh, the Wiener Wasteland, and the Sausage Sea, and the first player to make it to the frying pan wins.

Bacon Bar by Mo

How about Mo's Bacon Bar made with applewood smoked bacon that has been flavored with alder wood smoked salt, and then blended with deep milk chocolate. It has 41% cocoa and costs only $9.00. *Haven't tried one yet, but I have tried chocolate covered potato chips and they are very very good.*

Bacon Bra

Nuff said!

Bacon Candy Canes

Just in time to make your season jolly. *Tis the season.*

Bacon Candy Necklace

Here is a smokin' accessory to help you increase your popularity, the Bacon Candy Necklace. Comes complete with a gorgeous edible bacon medallion. *Mmmm*!

Bacon Cheddar Chips

Here is an interesting twist, potato chips on the outside and bacon with cheddar on the inside. Salty, crunchy, cheesy, and smoky, what more can a person want.

Butterz are hand formed and the bacon and cheddar are coated with an actual potato chip wrapped around. In fact, it's a thick potato chip batter, like Pringles. They also have other flavors made by B More Nutz in Baltimore and are available online.

Bacon Cheese Crickets

I would call them Creepy Crickets,
except for the bacon.

Bacon Coffin

"Yes, this is really real," wrote J&D owners Justin Esch and David Lefkow in an e-mail press release. "Bacon Coffins are finished with a painted Bacon and Pork shading and accented with gold stationary handles. The interior has an adjustable bed and mattress, a bacon memorial tube and is completed in ivory crepe coffin linens."

Bacon Cologne

Bacon perfume for the woman was first. Now bacon cologne (pronounced bac own) for men and women. Bacon classic is a blend of spicy maple, with bacon. Bacon gold is spicy citrus with bacon. Wow, what a great idea for those days when you do not have time for breakfast. Just think of it, citrus for her and maple for him or the other way.

Bacon Condoms

A condom that's patterned to look like a pinkish-red slab of bacon and is bacon flavored with the company's Baconlube. J&D foods claims the condoms are "made in America of the highest-quality latex and rigorously tested to help ensure the utmost reliability and safety for when you are *makin' bacon.*"

Bacon Crates

Mancrates http://www.mancrates.com/crates/bacon has a perfect gift for men. Crates contain Jeff's Famous Bacon Jerky, bacon salt, bacon sunflower seeds, bacon peanut brittle, bacon popcorn, bacon popped pop corn. It even comes delivered in a shipping box with a crowbar, or it can be shipped in a duct tape cocoon for the ultimate unwrapping experience.

Bacon Dental Floss

Bacon Deodorant

"J&D's POWER BACON™ Deodorant for when you sweat like a pig. Power bacon is designed specifically for people with active lifestyles. It provides 24 hours of bacon scent. For all day meat scented protection, apply liberally. Do not eat or leave exposed to sunlight. The company also makes bacon shaving cream, bacon sunscreen, and more.

Bacon Diet Coke

The Coca-Cola company supposedly tested its latest extension to the brand, Diet Coke with Bacon in test markets across the world including the UK, China, Australia and Africa in 2007. *Alas, great story, but it is a web inspired myth and untrue.*

Bacon Duct Tape

It is real duct tape with pictures of bacon rashers across the length. My niece Amy sent me some to hold stuff together.

Bacon Effervescent Drink Tablets

Just add two bacon drink tablets to any drink and you too can enjoy the sensation of sizzle in liquid form. Effervescent bacon tablets in water explode in a shower of fizz and delicious bacon flavor. They make regular water taste better than vitamin water. Oooh, drop some in vodka or drop some in hot chocolate for ultimate bubbly chocolate bacon.

Bacon Goldfish

Bacon cheddar puffs sound good to me.

Bacon Guitar

Here is something you don't see every day. Sounds OK, but would smell better if it was cooked. For those who might be interested, link that shows how you can make your own, along with a song from the author, "Bacon Loves Blues." *Am sure you can play some crispy sounds on this instrument.*

Bacon Gumballs

My way-much-older brother gave me some of these tasty treats. Everyone who tries some says that they are - um - ah - interesting. Some folks didn't even spit them out.

Bacon Gummies

Yummy gummy bacon. great to snack on at the office to keep that bacon fix on all day.

Bacon Hand Sanitizer

Bacon Hot Sauce

This will heat up your meals.

Bacon Inhaler

Some turn to transdermal pig patches, but you may have longer-lasting results with the Bacon Inhaler. Two or three puffs of the baconated vapor will satisfy your body's cravings for bacony protein anywhere or anytime. It is like bacon fresh air.

Bacon Jerky

It's only natural that the company that invented Bacon Jerky™ has the largest selection of bacon and pork jerkies in flavors like Jalapeno, Honey BBQ, Cajun, Maple, and Summer BLT.

Bacon Jigsaw Puzzle, 1,000 pieces

This is a real challenge to put together.

Bacon Jim Beam Mustard

Bacon Lottery Ticket

Actually a few states, notably New Hampshire and Indiana so far, have begun using bacon as a way to increase lottery ticket sales. Check your own lottery for instant scratch 'n sniff fun. To promote the tickets, the New Hampshire Lottery drove a "bacon truck," and handed out free bacon samples.

Bacon Lube

For those intimate moments between the sheets.

Bacon Maple Potato Chips

These Kettle Chips are GMO-free, have no MSG or gluten, and are safe for people with peanut allergies. *Oh, and they taste good.*

Bacon Mints

What more could you ask for breath pleasing bacony mints. Makes kissing double the fun.

Bacon MMMvelopes

The quest for all things tasting like bacon continues with another new invention. This time it is envelope glue that tastes like bacon.

It is time to show your good taste, but don't over-lick the bacon flavored glue on the envelopes designed in subtle classic bacon style. Almost *takes the pain out of paying bills.*

Bacon Mouthwash

Procter & Gamble's Scope brand ran Facebook postings as well as print ads for a new bacon-flavored Scope mouthwash. "Kills 99.9% of bad breath germs with 100% bacon taste," the ad claims. "The country's obsession with all things bacon led us to poke a little fun at ourselves," says Proctor and Gamble.

Bacon Paste

Only available in the UK, but looks like a great product.

Bacon Playing Cards

A great way to spice up your game and distract your opponents.

Bacon Popcorn

It is better than you might think. When we were growing up, our mother always had a jar of bacon grease on the stove. She used it to cook many things and also to pop popcorn (the old fashioned way, in a pan) and it gave the popcorn a hint of bacon flavor. Now you can buy microwave popcorn with the bacon flavor already in it. *I know she would approve.*

Bacon Potato Chips

Who's Your Daddy makes handmade bacon potato chips. These bacon fries below are from Tayto.

Bacon Ranch Popcorn

Seasoned with old-fashioned buttermilk, and an all natural, irresistible bacon flavor popcorn with smoky finish. Flavorful all natural, gluten free snack with whole grains and zero trans fat.

Bacon Rimshot Salt

A great taste add-on for your favorite drink. Try a margarita with a flavorful rimshot.

Bacon Retro Wall Clock

For all you clock watchers at the office. Guaranteed to make you hungry all day.

Bacon Roses

Would a rose by any other name smell as sweet? It would if it was bacon. There are many recipes online to make your own. The Bard's question is finally answered.

Bacon Rub

Here is a grilling favorite, a dry rub with a twist. Bacon Rub allows you to give nearly any meat a bacon-wrapped flavor simply by rubbing on this mix of herbs, spices, and brown sugar.

It is all-natural, Kosher, vegetarian friendly, and zero fat. *Rub me baby!*

Bacon Salt

You probably know that I enjoy a good piece of bacon every now and then, and this new product grabbed my attention. The ad says it is zero calorie, zero fat, vegetarian, and kosher seasoning that makes everything taste like bacon.

Bacon flavored salt is low in sodium, zero calories and fat, this product allows bacon-lovers everywhere to enjoy all the flavor of their beloved treat without a side of guilt.

Sprinkle it over eggs, potatoes, meats, baked beans, soups, salads, and sandwiches. It is available in many flavors for every occasion. *Alas, I read the ingredient list and there is nothing close to bacon in the list.*

Bacon Scarf

It's called the "Fou Lard" and it's a 100% silk scarf that is digitally printed to look like bacon. This is the brain child of Swiss artist, Natalie Luder, and is apparently meant to symbolize man's dominance over animals, or something.

Anyway, the whole thing's available for purchase if you want to remind people that you eat bacon and/or hunt pigs, which is great, because the gift-giving season is upon us.

Also worth knowing: the name of the scarf, Fou Lard, is a play on words. It comes from the French word for silk (foulard), which is made up from the words fou (crazy) and lard (fat). The foulard, or the silk crazy fat. Because. . . you know, bacon.

Bacon Scented Candles

How about some Bacon, or Pancake, or Coffee scented candles. *Smells so goooood! Gives me a lardon!*

Bacon Scratch and Sniff Team Shirts

How about these for your favorite team. Caution, may lead to aggressive tackling and sniffing.

Bacon Shaving Cream

Be good to your beard, while you are being good to your olfactory sense.

Bacon Sneakers

These give a whole new meaning to odor eaters.

Bacon Snickers

Wow, these sound wonderful. Have not tried yet, but state fair is coming soon.

Bacon Socks

Go ahead, walk proud. Cross your legs during negotiations and destroy your opponent, just like women do.

Bacon Soda

It finally happened, Jones Soda has come out with a vegetarian friendly and kosher bacon soda. How's that for an oxymoron? Another one below is Lester's Fixins bacon soda

Bacon Suckers

Lolliphile packs plenty of pucker into their lollipops. It offers a bacon lollipop with a kick of caffeine. According to Lolliphile, "We invented the Maple Bacon Lollipop, and now we've improved it: we've made it the bacon-y equivalent of an energy drink, adding two cups worth of caffeine to the already time-tested wonder of organic, sustainably farmed bacon and delicious Vermont maple syrup."

Bacon Sunflower Seeds

Sunflower seeds with bacon salt. How could that not be extra healthy!

Bacon Sriracha Jerky

Trader Joe's is selling Sweet Sriracha Bacon Jerky, Oh, yes!

Bacon Sriracha Lollipops

Bacon Soap

My way-much-older brother gave me some of this and now I can't keep the women away. Great way to wake up with a morning shower and bacony aroma.

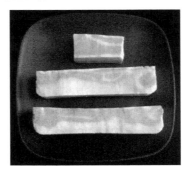

Bacon Squeeze

How about a squeeze bacon and squeeze cheese sandwich. Vilhelm Lilleflāsk's Squeez Bacon® is fully cooked 100% bacon. Due to the patented electro-mechanical process by which Squeez Bacon® is rendered, it requires no preservatives or other additives. Each serving is as healthy as real bacon, and equivalent to four premium slices of bacon - It was a great April Fools Day joke, but then someone made it real.

Bacon Squeezins

The Bacon Squeezins Water Bottle is a stainless steel water bottle with screenprinted graphic of Mr. Bacon enjoying a refreshing drink of delicious liquid fat. It holds 20 oz (600 ml)

Bacon Sunscreen

Too hot to handle, rub some of this stuff on. *Caution, may make your tan streaky.*

Bacon Tape

Like rashers on a roll.

Bacon Toothpaste

You will never need to wash away that fresh bacon smell from your mouth again.

Bacon Toothpicks

These should come in handy for parties. Stretch that bacon flavor all day.

Bacon Tux

You can actually buy one on the web, along with a bacon tie and pocket square.

Bacon Wallet

Your ATM will drool when you slide in your bacon scented cards.

Raleigh Bacon Bar

It features a layer of bacon, salt, and fresh caramel on top of pecan nougat, all wrapped up in a thin coating of delicious dark chocolate. The bacon flavor is subtle and blends deliciously with the salted caramel.

Manly Bacon Cupcakes

Looks like someone has kicked it up a notch. One shop has come up with some new manly cupcakes and they are selling like, um, bacon. For the Love of Cake's 'mancakes' feature such ingredients as beer and bacon, with no pink sprinkles.

The macho cupcakes are part of a new trend that is seeing the once dainty desserts reinvented for an audience that drinks milk straight from the carton. They are a tongue-in-cheek response to the apparently too-prissy offerings that dominate display cases. At Butch Bakery in New York, the 12 available flavors.

Bacon Watch

From the ad - "The irresistible allure of bacon (streaky bacon, as they call it in the UK) has crossed over into the world of fashion. Each watch has a 1-1/8" round clock face and straps that look like delicious slices of bacon. Vinyl strap, metal casing. Batteries included." *Looks tacky, but fun.*

Bacon Lance

Popular Science writer Theodore Gray recently embarked on an experiment of supreme bacon significance. He created a "bacon lance" which is a form of "thermal lance" — a device typically made of iron to cut through scrap metal. This is something you just have to see to believe. Flaming bacon cutting through metal.

Tactical Canned Bacon

Whether you fight zombies or terrorists, or zombie terrorists, your military rations wouldn't be complete without a couple of cans of

Tac Bac. With about 54 slices of delicious bacon per can, you will always be prepared for whatever life throws your way. Each can has a 10 year shelf life, but I doubt it would last that long in my bunker.

Reddi Bacon

Here is one of the very few bacon products that did not sell – pop a packet of the foil-wrapped processed meat into your toaster, wait a few minutes, and enjoy piping hot Reddi-Bacon.

What could possibly go wrong? A lot of things: An absorbent pad in the packet intended to soak up the grease tended to leak inside the toaster, creating an obvious fire hazard as well as a greasy toaster. The product was pulled before being released nationally.

American Chemical Society

Everyone loves bacon, but it's more than the smoky flavor that draws us back to those crispy pig parts again and again: It's also that distinct bacon-y aroma. Having already tackled the chemistry of Sriracha and the chemistry of pepper, Reactions—a video series by the American Chemical Society (ACS), just released a video that details why we love the smell of bacon.

As they point out, some of us even bathe ourselves in bacon scent. What makes the smell so good is the Maillard reaction (responsible for giving browned foods their desirable taste) that occurs when bacon is exposed to heat.

That reaction between sugars and amino acids mixes with the melting fats that are so plentiful in bacon and the result, as we know, is irresistible.

Bacon USB

Bacon goes high tech with this little goodie. The only thing better would be an app that made it smell like bacon. *That's a flashy flash drive.*

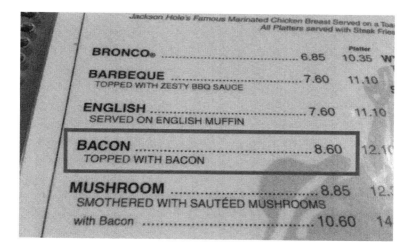

Bacon does not clog your arteries, it reinforces them.

PIGS IN THE MEDIA

Porky Pig from Looney Tunes fame. The inspiration was Joe Cobb, Joe in the "Our Gang/Little Rascals" TV Series. Joe Cobb starred in 86 episodes of the series and played the ever smiling yet hapless stereotypical fat kid, who often sets up gags for the others.

During the early 1930s, Leon Schlesinger secured a contract to produce the Looney Tunes series for Warner Bros. He asked animator Robert Clampett and studio director Friz Freleng to design a new series of characters and suggested they do a cartoon version of the Our Gang films.

The first short, I Haven't Got a Hat, released in 1935 included: Beans the cat, Oliver Owl, a motherly cow named Mrs. Cud, and Porky Pig in the 'Joe' role. Porky quickly became the star. Porky's name came from Friz Freleng, who remembered two childhood friends and brothers nicknamed "Porky" and "Piggy" and decided to put the two names together. His trademark stutter comes from Joe Dougherty, the first voice actor to voice Porky. Joe had a very pronounced stutter and forced director Freleng to go through take after take of uncontrollable stuttering.

Eventually the studio realized the high production cost of the many hours of wasted material, and replaced Dougherty with Mel Blanc in 1937. By this time the stutter had become so associated with the character that Blanc was asked to use it to create a more precise comedic effect.

Porky's legacy continues with his signature line "Th-th-that's all folks" heard at the end of Looney Tunes episodes. The Warner Bros. other series, Merrie Melodies, which had always used "So Long, Folks" to close its short films, changed to the more catchy Porky line after opinion polls found most people better associated with it.

Miss Piggy from Muppets fame. We all know the story.

Babe, the Gallant Pig from Babe movie, 1995. Babe is an adaptation of Dick King-Smith's 1983 novel The Sheep-Pig, which tells the story of a pig who wants to be a sheepdog.

Blodwyn Pig performed brightly, but briefly at the cusp of the '60s and '70s. The brainchild of guitarist Mick Abrahams, who walked out on fame with Jethro Tull after a tiff with Ian Anderson, and multi-instrumentalist sax man Jack Lancaster, Blodwyn Pig cultivated a small but devoted following with their brash brand of bluesy jazz rock.

Pig Music

BLUES	
ARTIST	TITLE
Kenny Wayne	Pig Feet
Tiny Parham & The Blues Singers	Pig Meat Blues
Johnny Mac	When Pigs Fly
Big Bill Broonzy	Pig Meat Strut
Frankie "Half-Pint" Jaxon	Gimme a Pig Foot and a Bottle of Beer
Jumpin' Johnny Sansone	Pig's Feet and Tail Meat
Live Texas Blues	Wigs & Pigs Feet
Blind Boy Fuller	I Crave My Pig Meat
Georgia Tom Dorsey	Pig Meat Blues
Mae Glover	Pig Meat Mama
Georgia Tom Dorsey	Pig Meat Papa
Memphis Minnie	Pig Meat on the Line

Bob Log III	Pig Tail Swing
Ella Mae Morse	Pig Foot Pete
Chet Atkins	Pig Leaf Rag
Roosevelt Sykes	Little Sow Blues
Bo Carter	Pig Meat is What I Crave
Cannon's Jug Stompers	Pig Ankle Strut
ROCK	
Pink Floyd	Pigs on the Wing 1
Pink Floyd	Pigs on the Wing 2
Johnny Mac	When Pigs Fly
Baby Ray	Buster Pig Man
The Beatles	Piggies
Jerry Garcia	Pig in a Pen
COUNTRY & FOLK	
Burl Ives	The Sow Took the Measles
Pee Wee King	Cincinnati Flying Pig
Jerry Garcia	Pig in a Pen
JAZZ	

Lionel Hampton & His Orchestra	Pig Foot Sonata
John Coltrane	Hambone
Gene Krupa	Lyonnaise Potatoes And Some Pork Chops
Jazz Passengers	Pork Chop
Tiny Parham & The Blues Singers	Pig Meat Blues
REGGAE	
Midnite	Banking in the Pig
VOCALISTS & BROADWAY	
Betty Hutton	Pig-Foot Pete
Vic Damone	Cincinnati Flying Pig
Ruby Murray	The Old Pig Sty

Did you know there are **KPIG and KPYG** radio stations in California

United States of Bacon TV Show

Everyone has a bucket list of things to accomplish in their lifetime. They usually look a bit like this: hike the Appalachian Trail, visit Graceland, go on a New Orleans ghost tour, get pulled onto stage at a Vegas magic show, but Chef Todd Fisher hungers for experiences with a bit more meat to them. As a life-long restaurateur, Chef Todd's passion for palate pleasers has him questing for the best bacon, burgers, and steaks at not just eateries, but meat temples, across the nation in Destination America's new original series UNITED STATES OF FOOD, premiered with "United States of Bacon." Subsequent episodes include "United States of Burgers" and "United States of Steak", but who cares about that.

Throughout the series, UNITED STATES OF FOOD visits venues with the best and most innovative menus items in the nation. Making Chef Todd's "bucket list" are trail-blazing small businesses like the Bacon Bacon Truck in San Francisco and their traffic-stopping grilled cheese, which oozes bacon jam in addition to containing a few strips of the real stuff. A visit to NYC's famous Crif Dogs proves serendipitous as record-holding hot dog competitive eater Takeru Kobayashi is spotted among the crowd of diners tasting his first bacon-wrapped hot dog. Bacon is undeniably, irrefutably one of America's most favorite foods, but long gone are the days when all that greasy goodness was restricted to a measly side order at breakfast. Today, America is taking bacon to a wild, new extreme that has it popping up in meals and on menus you would never expect and in ways your taste buds have only dreamed. Chef Todd Fisher samples bacon burgers at Slaters 50/50 in Huntington Beach, Cal., learns how NYC's Crif Dogs crafts their bacon-wrapped hot dogs, and nibbles a bacon and chocolate ice cream sandwich at Big Gay Ice Cream.

Epic Mealtime

On September 29th, 2010, the YouTube channel Epic Meal Time was created. The cooking series consists of Harley Morenstein and friends who design food items or entire meals made primarily out of meat, specifically bacon. As of January 2012, the channel was the #11th most subscribed-to channel of all time. They published 70 views and have over 315 million views, with about 660,000 views a day. Now it has become a TV series where the guys continue their bacony, meaty antics.

Bacon Paradise

Travel Channel hosted an episode from the show "Food Paradise" entitled, "Bacon Paradise." The description: "Bacon Paradise; some use this delectable meat paired with eggs, waffles, and chicken and others as a tasty addition to burgers, salads, and chocolate, but one thing is for sure: Americans go hog wild for bacon."

Bacon Books

The '*Better Bacon Book*', was designed especially for tablets and is an interactive book that offers instructions on how to make your own bacon, build your own smoker, and find the best bacon to order. It also has 31 interactive bacon recipes and videos, 150 photos. *Now we know why the book sizzles. Disclaimer, I am not the author, although I wish I was.*

There is another bacon book, called '*50 Shades of Bacon*'. It is a recipe book with sexy titles, also on Amazon. *No, I am not the author of this one either.*

Another good one on Amazon - '*Bacon: A Love Story*: A Salty Survey of Everybody's Favorite Meat' by Heather Lauer. *Didn't write this one either,* but it contains many bacon and pig facts, along with some great recipes.

In *Sex and Bacon:* Why I Love Things That Are Very, Very Bad for Me, Sarah Katherine Lewis is a seductress whose observations about the interplay between food and sex are unusually delightful, sometimes raunchy, and always absorbing.

Note - I enjoy a good turn of the page and twist of plot. Some of these books link sex and bacon together and that is natural, because bacon is inherently sexy and sex can be very bacony. Even though I did not write these mentioned, I did write 49 other books in addition to this one. Many are humorous, some are serious, and some are profound. All are on Amazon, many are on Kindle, and some are in bookstores and libraries.

Ford Fiesta Bacon Wrap

From the Ford website - "Bacon has been a cornerstone of cuisine since ancient Rome. In recent years the cured meat has transformed from a food to a lifestyle – inspiring everything from medical supplies to plush toys. Now, with International Bacon Day just around the corner, Ford is savoring the salty side dish with the introduction of what is believed to be the first bacon-wrapped car – a 2014 Ford Fiesta. The pièce de résistance is the full 'Bacon Wrap' – 10 giant strips of delicious bacon rolled around the entire Fiesta for a carb-free ride." *Alas, it does not look like the wrap is available this year.*

Money cannot buy happiness, but it can buy bacon, which is luscious crispy happiness.

BACON EVENTS

Bacon Days - There are many groups claiming Bacon Days for various and sundry reasons. According to serious baconoligists, all agree on International Bacon Day, celebrated on the Saturday before Labor Day in the US as the largest bacon day celebration in the world.

Others come and go, but all are celebrated with porcine gustatory delights, fun, and good will toward fellow man.

International Bacon Day is held on the Saturday before Labor Day US (the first Monday of Sep.). Bacon Day is celebrated in the US, Australia, Canada, South Africa, Switzerland, and the UK, among others. According to some accounts, International Bacon Day was conceived in 2000 by the residents of the Craig, MA.

Not to be confused with **Harvest Bacon Day** in October. Harvest Bacon Day's main holiday is Harvest Bacon Day, which is held in October, on the Friday of the Canadian Thanksgiving weekend. From the official church of baconology, on Harvest Bacon Day, bacon is eaten at every meal, while we remember the very first pig that gave up his life to sustain ours, and allowed us as a species to discover bacon.

There is also a **Bacon Day** February 26.

Still another Bacon day is observed on December 30. It is described as the (US) **National Bacon Day** on December 30, 2015. "For those who are great fans of bacon but still haven't had enough of bacon in the International Bacon Day, the National Bacon Day, which is just one day prior to the New Year's Eve, will be the second chance to enjoy this yummy food."

At least one US Whole Foods Market declared August 20 as **National Bacon Lovers Day**.

WikiHow says, "International Bacon Day is the one day of the year for the world to come together and appreciate bacon in every way possible. Depending on the country, International Bacon Day is celebrated either on the first Saturday after the New Years in January, February 19th, or the Saturday before Labor Day."

None of the aforementioned are to be confused with National Pig Day, celebrated annually on the 1st of March and recognizes the domesticated pig.

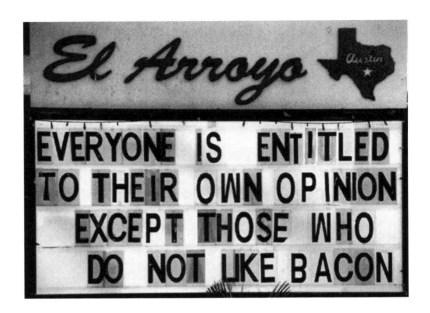

Recruiting With Bacon - Another reason why I love Google - It set up tables outside of Amazon headquarters to recruit new employees. It hired an ad agency to find a solution.

They set up a food cart outside of Amazon.com's headquarters and invited workers there to have some free bacon. A bunch of bacon lovers braved the rain for free strips of pepper bacon.

They also had toppings of spray cheese, peanut butter, maple syrup and chocolate sauce. Serious candidates even received a bacon air freshener. *How can you not appreciate the unique way to steal employees.*

Bacon Museum Exhibit - The Bacon Show at the Mew Gallery in Philadelphia was held in 2009. It featured a group exhibit curated by Mike Geno. The exhibition was a celebration of "the glory of bacon in all its sizzling, savory goodness," and brought together fine art painting, prints, photography, drawings, and inexpensive crafts (bacon soap art, magnets, etc). It included a "Mona Bacon" portrait made of bacon.

Bacon Festivals and Bacchanal

There are hundreds of bacon festivals each year around the world. The United States seems to reign supreme. I offer my listings as tribute and wish I could attend each one. Obviously they all have bacon in common and most have contests, samples, and generally a good time. *Maybe they will also begin to offer this book as a prize.*

Alferd (sic) Packer Bacon Party – Bacon, Bands, and Beer in Littleton, CO, US, Fundraiser for the Littleton Rotary Foundation

Austin, TX Bacon and Beer Festival - The 2nd Annual Austin Bacon and Beer Festival will be on Sunday, January 25 from 2:30–5 p.m., presented by Edible Austin in partnership with Eat Boston. The festival has previously sold out in Austin, Boston, Denver, San Francisco and Philadelphia. A portion of the proceeds benefit Capital Area Food Bank of Texas. This popular event showcases bacon-centric food prepared by bacon-loving chefs from Austin and Central Texas and pairing it all with craft brews. Can you ask for a Sunday afternoon better spent?

Bacon Bash – Royal Oak MI Farmers Market, 2015 Bacon Bash is held on April 17, 2015. On October 2, 2015 it hosts a **Baconfest.**

BaconCamp – 2014, First official BaconCamp in San Francisco From the site, "BaconCamp is an ad-hoc unconference inspired by BarCamp and dedicated to all things bacon. It is a fun event with discussions, dishes and interaction from attendees. Anyone with something to contribute or with the desire to learn is welcome and invited to join. When you come, be prepared to share and eat with BaconCampers. When you leave, be prepared to share it with the world." *I'm not going, but I shared anyway.*

On Thursday, September 5, the Iowa Bacon Board descended upon Iceland for the third year in a row to co-host the 2nd Annual **Reykjavik Bacon Festival**. The open-air event was held on Saturday, September 7 and attracted over 15,000 Icelanders to historic Skólavörðustígur in downtown Reykjavik. The festival offered over two tons of bacon, several pallets of beer, live music and a variety of bacon-inspired delicacies by the region's most prized chefs. Armed with Templeton Rye Whiskey, trays of bacon, and a gift from Iowa Governor Terry Branstad, the Iowa Bacon Board and their Icelandic counterparts were received and welcomed by Prime Minister Sigmundur Davíð Gunnlaugsson and U.S. Ambassador Luis E. Arreaga. "The Prime Minister acknowledged the importance of international bacon fellowship and praised all of us in spreading peace, joy and love – albeit in our own unique way. OHHHH, BACON!"

Big Bite Bacon Fest at the Queen Mary again in 2015, The Big Bite Bacon Fest returned, and it kicked August off in a crispy way during Aug. 1 and 2. The tasting event saw representation from Sweet Lou's BBQ Truck, OC Donut Bar, Hula's Hawaiian, and several other bacon-proud places and bacon-masterful chefs, plus more. Some delicacies include Bacon-Stuffed, PB&J, Fried Churro Hog Pockets, Bacon-Wrapped Chicken Drumsticks, bacon stuffed twinkies, bacon wrapped meatballs, and the Millionaire Bacon Bar with graham crackers, pretzels, potato chips, salted caramel, chocolate, coconut, butterscotch and peanut butter**.**

Bonnaroo - BaconLand and its bacon flights aimed to capitalize on the nation-wide love for all things bacon. "It came from me, being a bacon freak," Black said. "We wanted to start it off as a vendor to test the idea, before possibly opening a restaurant. Everyone loves bacon, but there really aren't a whole lot of bacon-themed restaurants. We did bacon tastings of 50 or 60 kinds and wound up using a beloved local brand, Benton's, on all of the sandwiches."

BaconLand, there was Hamageddon, a 4,000-pound, 22-foot-long steel pig that breathed fire from its nose and back end and housed a whole hog roasting in its nucleus. "We call him Henri," Black said. "I always wanted to own a teacup pig and name him that."

Bacon Party and Live Badger Raffle – Biennial event in Neenah, WI, US. Next event is September 19, 2016.

When it comes time for gifts for me, I hope someone keeps this web site in mind. It is a bacon-of-the-month club gifts. How better to tell that certain someone that you are thinking of them every month of the year. Bobby Flay's father bought him a one year subscription. *Bacon is almost as good as potato chips. OK, OK, sorry. I just had to say it.*

Bacon Barter - They have finally done it. Driving across country with no money and no credit cards. Josh Sankey was freeloading his way across the US armed with nothing more than a truckload of bacon. Oscar Mayer supplied enough bricks of Butcher Thick Cut Bacon fill his refrigerated truck. Sankey literally hauled a trailer full of 3,000 pounds of bacon from New York to L.A., going coast to coast with zero cash, cards, or checks. He relied on the goodness of Americans and the goodness of bacon. He offers bacon to finagle whatever he wants from whomever he wants and so far it worked. *I imagine when he needs a snack, he just throws a few rashers on the engine block to heat them up.*

Twitter has **@BaconFestCanada** - You had me at bacon. Sept. 24th, 2011, Calgary **@TheCanuckFoodie** Dude were you there? Thousands if people had a great time. Don't be hatin'. Love, Bacon.

Double Bacon Corn Dog - The Iowa State Fair has a new treat. The Campbell's Concessions' Double Bacon Corn Dog. The recipe - Wrap a hot dog in bacon, deep-fry it, dip it in 'bacon-bit-enriched' batter and deep fry it again.

The 2015 **Ultimate Bacon Brisket Bomb** features 8 oz. of fresh brisket trimmings infused with a light jalapeno cheese, blended with seasonings, and then wrapped in bacon. It is then smoked and lightly sauced in a homemade Sweet Chili BBQ Sauce. Update, The Ultimate Bacon Brisket Bomb took top honors in the fair's 2015 New Food Contest.

Bacon Queen 2012 - The Feb. 18 Blue Ribbon Bacon Festival is already sold out. Ten women are still competing for the title of Bacon Queen 2012 and moved on to the live Bacon Queen pageant, Feb. 16 at Johnny's Hall of Fame, Des Moines. The judges crowned the Blue Ribbon Bacon Festival Bacon Queen. Might not sound like much, but for a state that raises 30 million pigs a year, pork is a big deal. Des Moines also hosts the annual international **World Pork Expo** in June.

Bacon Palooza - Sorry I missed that one. A few weeks ago in New York, an event was held. It was billed as a "Meaty" FUNDRAISER TO HELP KIDS WITH AUTISM!' and "The Power of Bacon has been harnessed for the Forces of Good!" Come on, admit it. We all share the goodness of bacon. *MMM* - They even had a bacon eating contest, naturally.

Portland Bacon Fest - The second annual Portland Bacon Fest was held on August 21 and was a huge success with all things bacon available. *Another city catches the bacon wave.*

Camp Bacon - During June, a number of people from around the country descended into Ann Arbor, Michigan for Camp Bacon (not to be confused with San Francisco BaconCamp).

It started early Saturday morning as they sat down to breakfast under a big white tent. Their plates were piled high with hickory-smoked bacon from Edwards of Surry, Va.; long pepper bacon from Arkansas' Ham I Am; and applewood-smoked bacon from Nueske's in Wisconsin; plus bacon scones and a slice of bacon-apple coffee cake for good measure.

Many luminaries of the bacon world were there plus new rising stars from California to New York. "It's a thinking person's bacon camp," said Ari Weinzweig, co-founder of Ann Arbor's Zingerman's, which hosted the event. Camp Bacon was Weinzweig's attempt to re-channel bacon enthusiasm. *I didn't know it needed to be re-channeled.*

Bacon Bash - Do not forget to attend the annual bacon bash if you are in Pittsburgh. The Harris Grill hosts the event. Fun events and even some Maple Bacon Gelato will be on hand. Last year almost two hundred people made it to the event.

State Fairs and Bacon Fests

Texas State Fair - Butch Benavides won a trophy for his fried bacon cinnamon roll on a stick. Texas fried fireball," he explains.

That's pimento cheese, bacon, pickles, got some cayenne pepper. He rolls the orbs in egg wash and spicy bread crumbs.

2013 Blue Ribbon Bacon Festival - The date has been set for the 2013 Blue Ribbon Bacon Festival in Des Moines. On February 9, 2013, Blue Ribbon Bacon Festival, the World's premier bacon festival, provided temporary asylum for Icelandic bacon refugees fleeing their homeland in fear of the impending European bacon crisis.

Enid, Oklahoma had its first Baconalia event in 2010 with hog calling, bacon eating contest, and much more.

First Annual Iowa Bacon Expo, **Ames, Iowa** October 19, 2013 Features all things bacon, t-shirts, bacon deserts, exhibits, music, Miss Bacon Pageant, bacon eating contest, and demonstrations. It billed itself as the only student-run baconfest in the nation. It is a bit less ambitious and cheaper than the monster Annual Blue Ribbon Bacon Festival held in Des Moines, Iowa, which sold out its tickets in three minutes. "The love of bacon is unwavering," said Jake Swanson, originator of the Expo.

Great American Bacon 5k **North Miami, FL** A fun, well organized, bacon themed, 5k fun run. Bacon Bash After-Party: free bacon, music, awards, bacon themed food trucks, bacon beer, bacon ice cream, vendors, merchandise and a free ice cold beer waiting for you at the finish line (location and age permitting).

Feb 14 week - Bacon Week at the Tropicana Casino and Resort in **Atlantic City, N.J.**

Dewey Beach, DE Bacon Fest – General Admission - 2nd Wave Entry 4/23/16 Dewey Beach Bacon Fest & 4/24/16 Rehoboth Beach Bacon Fest. General Admission includes: Scorecard, Special Offers, Discounts on Lodging and will be the 1st General Admission wave to sample the bacon at each location both days.

Easton, PA bacon fest Nov 7 - 8, 2015. Web site has no details yet, but the words bacon fest caught my attention.

Heavy Seas Beer & Bacon Festival **Halethorpe, MD** - Heavy Seas hosts this all you care to taste beer and bacon affair at the actual brewery with 10+ restaurants, bacons from all over and live music.

Lehigh Valley Bacon & Brews Bash – "Bacon Days" is inspired by the success of the IronPigs' brand-new bacon-themed uniforms. The IronPigs' new on-field Saturday cap, emblazoned with a strip of bacon across the front, was Minor League Baseball's top-selling cap in 2014 and has been sold to all 50 states as well as over a dozen countries on four continents making Coca-Cola Park the unofficial, "Home of Bacon."

Baltimore, MD, Maryland Bacon Festival - Indications are that it did not go as well as expected. *What - Say it ain't so Joe!*

Beer bacon music: take 2 May 16, 2015, **Frederick, MD** fairgrounds (Maybe to ease the bad feelings from Baltimore)

Beer Bourbon and BBQ Festivals – Various States and cities, with bacon eating contests and bacon tasting NY, FL, VA, MD, NC

Iowa State Fair The Bacon Daddy of bacon events - It added a number of new items during 2015, including *Ultimate Bacon Explosion*, 8 oz. of fresh brisket trimmings infused with a light jalapeno cheese, blended with seasonings, and then wrapped in bacon. It is then smoked and lightly sauced in a homemade Sweet Chili BBQ Sauce. It is also 100% gluten-free.

Wisconsin State Fair - Wisconsin paid tribute with its latest on-a-stick creation, **the Fat Elvis**: a peanut butter cup dunked in banana batter, then deep-fried, and served with bacon on top.

Even the venerated **Waldorf Astoria** has its own Baconalia: A Celebration of the Waldorf Astoria's Bacon.

Kempton, PA Bacon/Brew Fest

New York, NY Bacon and Beer Classic

Naples FL (Hodges University) Bacon Fest

Norfolk, VA Bacon Fest

Philadelphia, PA Pennsylvania Bacon Festival

Philadelphia, PA Bacon and Beer Festival

Springfield, MO Ozarks Bacon Fest

Kansas City, MO Bacon-Fest

Sacramento, CA Bacon Fest

Cary, NC and Woodbridge, VA Beer and Bacon Festival

Washington, D.C. Capital Bacon Fest

Coshockton, OH Appalachian Bacon Nation A Celebration of Bacon

Albuquerque, NM Southwest Bacon Festival

Guilford, VT Brattleboro Baconfest: Bacon, Blues and Brews

Los Olivos and San Diego, CA Bacon and Barrels

Bentonville, Arkansas Bacon Bowl

Chicago, IL Baconfest Chicago

Glendale, OH Beer Wine Food: Bacon Edition

Long Beach, CA Big Bite Bacon Fest

Ybor City, FL Baconalia Festival

Bacon Palooza

Many fundraisers feature women in designer gowns and men in tuxes, but over the weekend in New York City's SoHo neighborhood held a different kind of charity event: The Bacon-Palooza.

John Ordover, who runs the SoHo Gallery for Digital Art, says he decided on the bacon theme because - except for those with a religious requirement against pork - everybody he knows loves bacon. "It crossed all the social lines of rich, poor, happy, sad, outgoing, introverted," he says. "If there is one thing that everyone can agree on, it's bacon."

The dress was casual, the people were young, and the cause was to raise money for kids with autism.

The event had everything bacon: bacon the movie, bacon the musical, bacon songs, bacon art, bacon products, and, of course, bacon food and drink. There was balsamic bacon-wrapped shrimp with chipotle sauce, bacon sweet potato hash, bacon-wrapped dates, bacon dipped in chocolate, to mention a few.

Drinks included a BLT with bacon vodka, tomato juice and a sprig of lettuce, and a bacon egg cream, which consisted of bacon vodka, chocolate syrup, seltzer and milk.

The bacon burlesque striptease, where the pasties were bacon. There were Gregorian chants based on bacon recipes sung by the Sugar-Cured Singers, and there were movie clips and musical offerings. There were also bacon-related cartoons and art on the walls.

Bacon Fueled Motorcycle - Hormel created a motorcycle that is fueled by bacon grease for its journey from Minnesota to the San Diego Big Bite Bacon Fest. Needless to say, a great time was had by all.

The Oakland Athletics have a **Bacon Tuesday** for the fans, dedicated to all things bacon.

The Great American Bacon Race The Tastiest 5k on Earth. Run 3.1 miles and eat free bacon along the way at bacon stations. The races are annual events and there are three races in Florida during August, September, and October 2015.
http://americanbaconrace.com/

Bacon Skates

These photos below were taken in November 1931 in Chehalis, Washington at the town's Egg Festival. The occasion was a try to break the world record for largest omelette. Two women tied bacon to their feet and skated around the warming skillet to grease it. Then a team of chefs cracked and beat 7,200 eggs and made a breakfast delight.

I suffer from interminable bacon lust.

BACON ON THE GO

Bacon Theme Restaurants

In addition to virtually all fast food places offering something with bacon, now there are specifically bacon themed restaurants popping up all over the US, from New York to California.

Nine-unit **Arooga's Grille House & Sports Bar** chain based in Harrisburg, Pa., is mounting its 2015 bacon blitz by adding a new line of Bacon Grind Burgers: patties that are 65% ground steak and 35% ground bacon.

Bacon (Austin, Texas) - Bacon was "started with an idea that we wanted to make bacon better," says partner Jed Taylor, who debuted the restaurant over International Bacon Weekend a few years ago. It begins with preparing everything in-house, allowing the crew to get creative with signature flavors. Their most popular is Tabasco, and they also do varieties like Chinese five-spice, coconut curry and wasabi. It's available straight-up or worked into any number of dishes, including their BLT, "double grind" burger (bacon in the patty) and bacon house salad.

The Works Gourmet Burger Bistro, Canada builds on a promotion it ran during 2014, "Believe in Baconism II" It introduced three specialty burgers, two sides, and a shake, all blessed with bacon.

Six Degrees of K'vin Bacon has bacon six ways: an 8-oz. bacon and beef patty topped with Canadian bacon, smoked bacon, bacon ketchup, bacon-roasted garlic aïoli and bacon sticks, plus lettuce and tomato.

An updated favorite is the Getting Piggier With It: the 8-oz. bacon and beef patty with Canadian bacon, Cheddar, smoked bacon, bacon ketchup and crunchy onion strings.

The When Pigs Fly has a bacon-and-beer-seasoned chicken breast that's grilled and topped with smoked bacon, house-made bacon jam an onion ring, lettuce and tomato.

On the side are bacon-wrapped Cheddar-and-potato balls with bacon roasted-garlic aïoli and bacon sticks. More bacon goodies include fresh-cut fries covered with bacon seasoning and topped with bacon roasted-garlic aïoli, bacon and green onions. The Bacontella Shake with Nutella blended with smoked bacon, Canadian ice cream, and topped with whipped cream and, bacon.

Sage General Store (Long Island City, N.Y.) - "People always do pairings of wines. Why can't you do that with bacon?" That simple, glorious thought process is what led Leslie Nilsson, owner of Queens' Sage General Store, to launch her popular all-bacon weekend brunch. It serves three bacon varieties — Neuske's, from Wisconsin, Dewig's, from Indiana, and Ham I Am!, from Texas.

It offers a three-course $25 bacon celebration, which also features dishes like five-cheese bacon mac 'n' cheese and a double chocolate bacon brownie, with bacon bits in the batter.

Cousin's Grubhouse (Philadelphia, Pa.) - In early 2013, Jim Lord and Bill Schmidt took over a luncheonette in Deep South Philly and converted it into Cousin's Grubhouse. It has bacon-centric options for days. Big sellers include bacon-wrapped jalapeno tater tots, a bacon-wrapped, chili-cheese-smothered "Heart Attack Dog" and bacon-infused pancakes and the "Grubhouse Porker," a sandwich piled with bacon, fried bologna, ham, and barbecue root beer pulled pork.

Bacon Bacon (San Francisco, CA) - Jim Angelus launched Bacon Bacon, a cafe with the same name as the food trucks, but it was closed in connection with a neighborhood clash that earned national attention. He since was officially granted permission to reopen and is hunting for a second permanent space and also signed a contract for a second truck.

Phylis Johnson-Silk, who lives around the corner made signs that said, "Bacon rules!" and "Really? You complained to the cops that you smelled bacon?" Jim printed up shirts that read, "Smell this."

La Quinta is getting on the bacon bandwagon. It bagan showing commercials for La Quinta with the star 'bring home the bacon'.

Brutus Restaurant (Montreal, Canada) – Every item on the menu contains bacon.

The folks in San Francisco were delighted that, for a limited time, they had bacon delivered to them. Floral delivery startup **BloomThat**, with the help of food truck **Bacon Bacon,** delivered succulent strips of bacon to their door (or bar stool).

During the week ending Sunday, June 15, 2014 it sent some sizzle to someone special. For $15, the company's arranged for the Bacon Bacon truck to deliver six strips of high-quality cured bacon to anyone located in the San Francisco area.

Bacon Happy Hour at The Macintosh, Charleston, S.C. - Every weekday from 5 to 7 p.m., guests taste pork belly. Chef Jeremiah Bacon (his real name) features a pig-centric dish of the day, such as pork-belly lettuce wraps with spicy garlic sauce or pigs in a blanket with buckwheat pancakes, crispy pork belly and roasted tomato aioli.

24 Diner, (Austin, TX) – It serves bacon, avocado and charred *poblano* pepper sandwich with smoked aioli.

In an exclusive upscale **Beverly Hills hotel bar called simply £10**. The setting has the center of the table with the bacon in the glass along with the other bar munchies. *A bit of class in the glass.*

Bacon Trucks

A number of cities have seen the coming of food trucks dedicated to all things bacon. A few of them include:

Bacon Bacon, San Francisco, California

Bacon Boys Truck, Las Vegas, Nevada

The Bacon Wagon in Fort Worth, Texas

The Caveman Truck, Indianapolis, Indiana

Bacon Lover's Truck Addison, Texas

The Bacon Truck, Boston, Massachusetts

The Bacon Truck, Detroit, Michigan

The Bacon Trolley, St. Paul, Minnesota

Bacon MANia Truck, Orange County, California (and Northern CA)

Bacon Boss, Tampa, Florida

Bacon on Wheels, New Jersey

Lard Have Mercy, Austin, Texas

Pig on the Street, Vancouver, British Columbia

Pig Viscous, Austin, Texas

Cap't Bacon Truck, Provo, Utah is holding a Kickstarter to raise enough money to get the truck on the road (to date, it had one backer with $28.00 pledge). *Not too encouraging.*

Bacon Tragedy

A Chicago-bound Amtrak train collided with a tractor-trailer carrying 70,000 pounds of bacon June 5, 2015, spewing meat all over the tracks in Wilmington, Ill.

None of the 203 passengers were seriously injured when the Texas Eagle train ran through the truck. The truck had been sitting on the tracks, and the driver was able to flee the vehicle before it was hit. It was not immediately clear if the driver was injured.

Luckily there was no fire or the crowds scooping up the succulent sizzle would have stopped traffic for miles.

Bacon Chocolate Cake

Woods Jupiter, Tiger Woods' eight million dollar Jupiter, Florida sports bar eatery, has bacon chocolate cake on the menu and folks have been raving about it. *Keep them happy Tiger.*

Bacon Ninja

Japan Burger King offers Black Ninja with black bun and fully loaded with a whopper patty, onions, lettuce, mayonnaise, hash browns, and a huge bacon slab.

Bacon Pig on a Stick

Linton Hopkins' menu at Restaurant Eugene in Atlanta: three hunks of 24-hour braised pork belly, crisped, then threaded on a stick and gilded with barbecue sauce.

Slater's 'Merica Burger

California burger chain Slater's 50/50 has a menu that features a burger made of 100 percent ground bacon and comes topped with a slice of thick-cut bacon, bacon island dressing, and bacon flavored cheddar cheese. It's only non-bacon topping is a sunny-side-up egg. Alas, it is only offered in July and it is called 'Merica.

Its regular flagship burger is made of half ground beef and half ground bacon.

Slater's offers several other bacon-themed goodies, including a bacon brownie and the Bakon Mary, a twist on the Bloody Mary cocktail featuring bacon-infused vodka, a rim of bacon salt and a slice of thick-cut bacon as garnish.

Bacon at Fast Food Places

Since I began putting this bacon tome together, Denny's has also chosen to describe its "bacon love fest" and adding a number of menu items that include bacon, such as bacon meatloaf, bacon maple sundae, and more. I commend Denny's for its insight.

According to Denny's History of Baconalia, "Very little is known about the origins of Baconalia, but from what bacon scholars have pieced together from strips of ancient texts it was one heck of a bacon lovefest. Some believe Baconalia to be the last vestige of the Baconites, a Paleolithic tribe of fun, bacon loving people that roamed across land masses with large frying pans in search of bacon."

Denny's has revived its version of Baconalia for 2015 with items, such as Maple Bacon Sundae, a Maple Bacon Milkshake, a Salted Caramel Brownie Sundae with Bacon, BBQ Bacon Mac 'n' Cheese Bites and Bacon Pepper Jack Tilapia.

- Carl's Jr. took bacon to the max by rolling out the X-Tra Bacon Cheeseburger with four strips of bacon on a char-broiled beef patty.

- Burger King introduced a Bacon Sundae, soft serve drizzled with chocolate fudge, caramel sauce, and bacon crumbles.

- Red Robin rolled out a Beam-N-Bacon Boozy Shake with Jim Beam Maple Bourbon, bacon bits on top, and a candied strip of bacon for a stir stick. It offers a Southern Charm half pound Black Angus burger with candied bacon and coated in brown sugar made with honey BBQ sauce, cheddar cheese, red onions, lettuce, and mayo on a toasted ciabatta bun.

- Little Caesars began 2015 with a new pizza with 3 1/2 feet of bacon wrapped around the crust and bacon crumbles on top. It proudly says, "In Bacon We Crust!"

- Pizza Hut has a single topping choice with crust made with a blend of various cheese and bits of bacon. The Cheesy Bacon Stuffed Crust Pizza is available at participating Pizza Hut locations.

- Wendy's just introduced Baconator fries. It is a dish with French fries, bacon, shredded Cheddar cheese, and a cheese sauce.

- Wienerschnitzel has introduced Bacon Ranch Chili Cheese Fries feature chili cheese fries covered in creamy ranch sauce and bacon bits.

- Hardee's restaurants has a premium burger offering from Carl's Jr. and Hardee's. The Super Bacon Cheeseburger features a charbroiled beef patty, American cheese, mayonnaise, tomato, onion, lettuce and a super serving of bacon, with six full bacon strips woven together into a crispy bacon nest.

- Custom House in Barnstaple, North Devon, England sells its "15 Shades of Bacon" burger. The 2,500-calorie burger contains 15 types of bacon, unsmoked back bacon, unsmoked streaky bacon, smoked back and smoked streaky bacon, turkey bacon, prosciutto, mortadella, pancetta, a bacon burger, a sausage patty and chicken fried bacon, and to top it all off there's bacon crisps, baconnaise and bacon dusted chips.

- KFC has **a** "Double Down" bacon and cheese sandwiched between two pieces of fried chicken.

- Another from KFC Overall the bacony cheese bowl of goodness is hearty and savory with meat and carbs and dairy and fat all mixing together.

- Arcapita, Bahrain, owns Church's Fried Chicken - (*that is likely why they took bacon off the menu*)

- Outback Steakhouse has an all-new bacon wrapped filet, a tender USDA 'Choice' petite filet wrapped in bacon then seasoned, seared, and paired with shrimp and scallops atop whole grain wild rice and served with a side of grilled asparagus.

- Subway has a double bacon, egg, and cheese breakfast sandwich.

- Krispy Kreme is partnering with a minor league baseball team in Wilmington to sell a bacon hot dog with raspberry jam covered with a Krispy Kreme doughnut as a bun. The Wilmington Blue Rocks, a single-A affiliate of the American League champion Kansas City Royals.

- Arooga's Grille House & Sports Bar chain based in Harrisburg, Pa., has a new line of Bacon Grind Burgers: patties that are 65% ground steak and 35% ground bacon.

- Wienerschnitzel has announced new versions of its most iconic menu item: the Chili Cheese Dog. Four of these new dogs include BACON: Buffalo Bacon, Triple Cheese Double Bacon, Bacon Ranch, and Loaded Bacon Street Dog.

- Jack In The Box is serving up breakfast for lunch in the form of their Hearty Breakfast Bowl with bacon.

- Hash House A Go Go has fried chicken and bacon waffles.

- Straw has donut burger with thick sliced bacon.

Bacon Lotto

And, if all else fails, go to New Hampshire and pick up a hundred new bacon lottery tickets. The New Hampshire state lottery is now offering a lottery ticket that smells like bacon. To help promote the tickets, the lottery handed out the scratch tickets and free slices of bacon.

The new tickets, which are scratch-n-sniff and read "I Heart Bacon," were released Jan. 5, 2015. Winners can take home $1,000 and the odds of making at least a dollar are one in 4.12 and the maximum payout is $1,000. Plus, it smells delicious.

The I Heart Bacon scratch ticket combines two things people love, the chance to win cash and the wonderful, enticing smell of bacon.

To promote the new ticket, bacon trucks will visit various locations in the state, handing out free samples of applewood smoked bacon as well as offering lottery tickets. As of this writing, more than 800,000 tickets were sold, making the bacon lottery the best selling $1 ticket.

Indiana has its own Bacon Lotto - In addition to the scratch n sniff ticket really smelling like bacon, the newest "Bringin' Home The Bacon" game offers players a chance to win a hefty supply of bacon for 20 years in addition to up to $10,000 in cash prizes, reports Consumerist. The 20 year supply of bacon allows gamers to receive $250 worth of bacon once a year for 20 years, or a lump sum of $5,000.

Bacon Places

There are eight states with nine towns named Bacon – Georgia, Idaho, Indiana, Missouri (2), Ohio, Texas, Virginia, and Washington. There are also multiple Cities and Counties named Bacon in the US.

Bacon Social Sites

Each social site seems to have its own public porcine personality.

I'm eating bacon

I like bacon

I have skills including eating bacon

This is where I eat bacon

Watch me eat my bacon

Here's a vintage photo of my bacon

Here's a recipe with bacon

I work for Google and eat bacon

I'm listening to music about bacon

Bacon Found in the Closet - Here is the headline, "*Third-degree burns, stitches for South Bend brothers-in-law fighting over frying pan.*" The argument led to the man cooking cornering the younger man into a closet and spilling hot grease on the younger man. The report said the 47-year-old then grabbed the pan from his attacker and hit him in the head twice. The 49-year-old was taken to an area hospital where he received 11 stitches before being arrested for assault, the report said. The man who received third-degree burns on his hands told police he did not wish to press charges. Police did report finding two pieces of bacon in the closet.

New Year Bacon - From Life Magazine Jan 1, 1940. "Frank Sinatra Ate Bacon When He Was Young. That Proves Bacon is Cool." *I didn't make this one up folks.*

Diamonds are the bacon of gems.

Viral Bacon Rant

According to The Daily Mail, a bacon lover's rant to Tesco after discovering his packet of smoked rashers was one short has gone viral during July, 2015. Ben Roberts wrote to the supermarket in a Facebook post to draw their attention to the "truly horrific moment" he encountered on a Sunday morning.

Good Evening Tesco,

I hope this post finds you well. I just wanted to draw to your attention a truly horrific moment I incurred on Sunday morning.

Now in our house it is pretty much tradition, or more like religion that we have bacon sandwiches in the morning on a weekend, as I am sure a lot of families are the same. After all bacon is the food of champions.

So here I am Sunday morning when suddenly I remember we don't have any bacon. I couldn't believe it! Heartbroken I was! I was on the brink of complete meltdown when I said to myself "Ben! It's okay! You can just pop down to your handy Tesco Local and pick up a delicious pack of Smoked, back bacon rashers!" Genius!

So I jumped in the car and drove my happy self down to Ye Olde Tesco. I park up, and skip my self into the shop and head for the meat section. I found the bacon, picked up the pack and thought that can go straight in my basket. Upon closer inspection at the checkout I read the front "7 Smoked Bacon Rashers" I chuckled to myself. 7. That's a strange number for a pack of bacon. I mean come on 7 is the number of days in the week, or the number of Sins but that is not a great number when it comes to rashers of bacon.

I should of walked away there and then I know but I didn't. Instead I thought it's ok, when I get home and have cooked the strange number of rashers I simply will have 4 and my other half can have 3. The thought of this made me smile. I will have the most bacon, because I deserve it.

Anyway, I get myself home, turn on the grill, line the tray with foil to avoid washing it and then ripped open the packet. I beamed from ear to ear as I proceeded to lay the bacon out.

"Suddenly.. I stopped. I began to feel myself sink again only this time it was worse. I looked down at the tray and then at the packet, then back at the tray and once more took a real good look at the plastic.

SHUT THE FRONT DOOR! There was only 6 rashers of bacon. 6. I could not believe it! Mortified! I called my other half into the kitchen but quickly dismissed her as she did not seem to understand the problem.

Well Tesco, let me explain in case you don't understand the problem. When I go to one of your stores and see 7 rashers of bacon for sale for £1.50 I expect 7 pieces! Not 5, or 6 or even 8 (well 8 is fine) but I expect 7! 7 of your finest rashers is what I wanted and I was sincerely disappointed.

I have attached photo evidence and basically what I want to know is what the bloody hell are you going to do about this cruel act of betrayal.

I look forward to your response and hopefully my additional rasher of bacon. ·

Tesco's reply - Jamie from the Tesco customer services department responded: "Well, it sounds like you've gone through a whirlwind of emotions for a Sunday morning.

"Like you my day, month, and year can be made by a top quality bacon butty. I'll eat them in all the conceivable varieties: with ketchup or with brown sauce. Sometimes, just sometimes, I'll treat myself to what I call the Jamie special. This requires three slices of bread, some Brie, some mild salsa, bacon (obviously), a dab of imagination, and a George Foreman grill (other lean mean grilling machines are available). As a fellow bacon fan I can fully understand your shock, disappointment and unadulterated anger at finding only six rashers in the packet.

As a gesture of goodwill, the supermarket said it would refund the price of the packet of bacon and passed on Mr. Roberts' details to the supplier.

Note - I did find Ben Roberts on Facebook, but could not find his letter on his pages or on the Tesco pages, or any reference to it. I pass this along anyway, just because it is fun.

True or not, I offer the bacon icon below to Ben.

Bacon Phone Apps

Bacon Live Wallpaper - It features fully animated bacon cooking right on your phone and when you touch the screen, it sizzles, including sound. *Alas, no bacon smell.*

Bacon Clock App - The bacon clock app can be yours for free or a donation of US$0.99. Instead of LED bars, the numerals are illuminated with enticing strips of crisp bacon that morph and roll over as the numbers advance. The way the bacon strips peel back, fold over, and hide and reveal themselves as the numbers tick up. Multiple backgrounds, including a stack of pancakes.

Baconnection: This bacon app has 3 main features:

Bacon Recipes: Hundreds of ways to make bacon! Prepare a bacon recipe a day for most of a year without eating bacon the same way twice. They have collected the best bacon recipes from Allrecipes.com, Taste of Home, and Every Day with Rachael Ray, and you get them all in this app.

Bacon Trivia: Find out how well you know bacon when you play the Bacon Bits quiz game. *This book should provide much needed assistance.*

Baconnection: You can connect any ingredient to bacon. Start with an ordinary ingredient and see how many recipes with overlapping ingredients you need to link it to a recipe containing bacon in six recipe steps or less.

Nova Bacon is an app from Microsoft garage. It follows what an alien out of food would do, go get more. Armed with a gigantic claw, you go down to Earth and fetch a pig while defending yourself from humans that aren't happy about contributing to your business. User can experience a variety of pigs while earning money to upgrade the various weapons available to you.

Bacon Freak's Bacon Is Meat Candy Club - Be surprised with a monthly box of two different 1lb packs of gourmet hog candy, deliciously marinated and spiced into a range of flavors like apple cinnamon, jalapeno, vanilla bourbon, pepper, and straight-up hickory smoked.

Bacon will make you live longer.

BACON SCULPTURE

Bacon Arpaio

Using cooked, pre-cooked, and uncooked varieties of bacon, a stable of sharp instruments, and a photo of "Joe," the bacon enthusiasts of Chow Bella in Phoenix got to the greasy work of assemblage, using layering techniques to first create the shape of the face, then tackling the porky parts like Sheriff Joe Arpaio's nose and chin.

Bacon Bieber

This is scary, but I am sure it was done with the best of intentions.

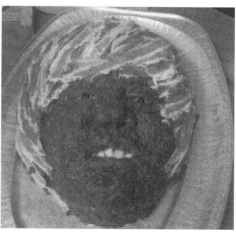

Bacon Conan Bust

Conan has a 200-pound bust of himself made entirely out of white chocolate and bacon. He made a comment during an interview that he would visit the Minnesota State Fair if he could get his body weight in chocolate covered bacon, which the Fair claims is a specialty of theirs.

Sculptor Linda Christensen labored over a 300-pound chunk of white chocolate for a full week before it was sent to O'Brien in California.

by Sara Bonisteel, Posted Aug 27th 2009 @ 12:30PM

205-pound bacon-hair-topped chocolate bust later, Conan O'Brien shows off the creation put together by No Name Premium Meats and butter sculptor Linda Christensen. "Tonight Show" host Conan O'Brien can rest easy knowing he's really made it in show business now that he's been recreated in bacon and white chocolate.

"I've long dreamed of this, but I never thought I'd see it happen," O'Brien said Wednesday as he unveiled the 200-pound bust on his program. While he said it was a gift from the Minnesota State Fair, Slashfood has learned that isn't exactly the truth behind the tasty tribute.

The bust was actually commissioned by a meat company, No Name Premium Meats, in St. Michael, Minn. The company commissioned the sculpture after O'Brien said in June that he would visit the Minnesota State Fair if they sent him his weight in chocolate-covered bacon, "which is one of the delicacies of the state fair," Kris Patrow, a publicist for No Name told Slashfood.

It took sculptor Linda Christensen a week to carve the likeness into a 300-pound block of white chocolate. In O'Brien's case, the makers decided not to use bacon for his skin. it was felt he was too pasty for bacon, so they carved him out of white chocolate. The bacon in this sculpture was saved for his red hair. O'Brien loved the sculpture. He said, "I've long dreamed of this, but I never thought I'd see it happen." Sadly, the bacon bust fell apart on the way out of the studio.

Bacon Kevin Bacon

J&D Foods teamed up with bacon-crafting blog What Do Bacon Do to create a Bacon Bust of Kevin Bacon. The pieced is made of a Styrofoam core covered in dried bacon bits. These were glued on the bust and covered with five coats of lacquer to ensure longevity. It measures 60 centimeters high and sits atop a marble base.

Artist Mike Lahue created the artwork, which was auctioned on eBay for charity Ashley's Team, a non-profit organization that helps children with cancer and their families. The charity was set up in J&D Foods co-owner Dave Lefkow's daughter's name. Four-year-old Ashley had been diagnosed with leukemia. It sold for $4,000 on ebay.

And another bacon Kevin Bacon masterpiece

Google has a 'degrees of bacon' number - Just type bacon number followed by the name of an actor or actress and you get the bacon number, as in six degrees of Kevin Bacon.

When I was young, we had Johnny Cash, Bob Hope, and Steve Jobs. Now we have no Cash, no Hope, and no Jobs. Please don't let Kevin Bacon die!

Crispi Bacon

A Utah woman angry at her ex-boyfriend admitted to police that she put a pound of bacon on a cookie sheet on top of his gas stove, turned the burner on "high," and left it there, allegedly in an attempt to burn the house down. Cameo Adawn Crispi, 32, pleaded guilty to reckless burning, attempted assault by a prisoner, and intoxication, all misdemeanors.

The man was not home at the time, but called the cops after getting fifteen calls and text messages from Crispi in less than an hour. The bacon was burned and smoking badly when officers arrived, with smoke pouring out the front door and Crispi clearly impaired. Crispi was arrested after a brief struggle; her blood alcohol content was found to be 0.346, which is more than four times what Utah considers "impaired."

Chris P. Bacon

When Chris's owner discovered that her piglet had been born with malformed hind legs, she took him to the vet to be euthanized, but rather than putting him down, the doctor decided to rescue Chris and have him fit for a special wheelchair. Dr. Len Lucero fashioned Chris's first wheelchair out of K'Nex toy parts, and when Chris outgrew it, upgraded to a device made by Handicapped Pets.

Now Chris has an active website that sells t-shirts (profits go to the Disabled American Veterans fund) and schedules pig appearances. *(Not to be confused with Christian Paul Bacon, the actor.*

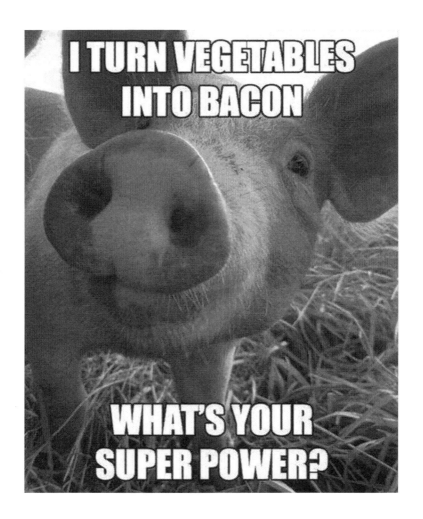

BACON STORY

A Dissertation Upon a Roast Pig

I remember the story by Charles Lamb (1775-1834), "A Dissertation upon Roast Pig." The story relates how a village in China had never eaten cooked meat. One day a child accidentally burnt down his father's house with three pigs trapped inside. The boy went into the now smoldering house and came upon a smell so grand that he had never smelled before. He reached down and touched the remains of one of the pigs. Because it was still hot, it burned his fingers and he immediately put them to his mouth for comfort and tasted the delicious flavor.

The word got out to the rest of the village, and soon everyone was herding the pigs inside and burning down their houses for the wonderful swine flavor.

The end of the story is that it took two centuries before they realized they could build a spit and did not need to burn down their whole house to enjoy the goodness of roast pig.

Toward the end of the story, he relates: "There is no flavor comparable, I will contend, to that of the crisp, tawny, well-watched, not over-roasted, crackling, as it is well called -- the very teeth are invited to their share of the pleasure at this banquet in overcoming the coy, brittle resistance -- with the adhesive oleaginous -- O call it not fat -- but an indefinable sweetness growing up to it -- the tender blossoming of fat -- fat cropped in the bud -- taken in the shoot -- in the first innocence -- the cream and quintessence of the child-pig's yet pure food -- the lean, no lean, but a kind of animal manna -- or, rather, fat and lean (if it must be so) so blended and running into each other, that both together make but one ambrosian result, or common substance."

Bacon is the nectar of the masses.

BACON IS BETTER THAN LOVE BECAUSE

- True love is found only once in a lifetime, but you can eat bacon seven days a week.

- Bacon is always faithful to you.

- Other people share their bacon with you.

- You can keep bacon in the fridge, but you cannot keep love in the fridge.

- Love wanes, but bacon never wanes.

- Love breaks your heart, but bacon stays in your heart forever.

- Bacon does not care what you do when you are not eating bacon.

- Bacon never complains.

- Bacon never talks back.

- Bacon affects your wallet only when <u>you</u> decide to spend money.

- Bacon is always there for holidays and you do not need to go visit bacon in-laws.

- You do not need to buy presents for bacon – it is a present for you.

- Bacon has no mother-in-law.

- You do not need to woo bacon, it woos you.

The liquid surrounding bacon in the pan is not grease,
it is the skillet crying tears of joy.

BACON QUOTES

- According to newlyweds Tricia Snider and Tom Watson, who tied the knot at the 2014 Blue Ribbon Bacon Festival in Iowa. Watson declared his love for his bride by saying, "She is second only to bacon." *the Des Moines Register*

- Seen on barbershop in London, England - "Some people won't try bacon for religious reasons. I won't try religion for bacon reasons."

- "I've long said that if I were about to be executed and were given a choice of my last meal, it would be bacon and eggs. There are few sights that appeal to me more than the streaks of lean and fat in a good side of bacon, or the lovely round of pinkish meat framed in delicate white fat that is Canadian bacon. Nothing is quite as intoxicating as the smell of bacon frying in the morning, save perhaps the smell of coffee brewing." — *James Beard (1903-1985)*

- "That ball is so far left, Lassie couldn't find it if it was wrapped in bacon." *David Feherty*, CBS and Golf Channel announcer

- Winter Olympian *Sage Kotsenburg*, tweeted Feb. 10, 2014 after winning the gold medal for slopestyle, "I wish the Sochi medals were made out of bacon."

- J&D Foods' co-owner *Justin Esch* told AOL: "Bacon makes everything better, including art."

- *Old Saying*, 'Butter Upon Bacon' it is an extravagance. "Are you going to put lace over the feather, isn't that rather butter upon bacon?"

- "Slap some bacon on a biscuit and let's go! We're burnin' daylight!" – John Wayne

Bacon Quotes from Homer Simpson

"(Lisa) "I'm going to become a vegetarian" (Homer) "Does that mean you're not going to eat any pork?" "Yes" "Bacon?" "Yes Dad" Ham?" "Dad all those meats come from the same animal" "Right Lisa, some wonderful, magical animal!"

"Porkchops and bacon, my two favorite animals."

"When you're in my house you shall do as I do and believe who I believe in. So Bart butter your bacon."

"Mmmm. Move over, eggs. Bacon just got a new best friend – fudge."

"Not again! First you took away my Philly Fudgesteak, and then my Bacon Balls. Then my Whatchamachicken. You monster!"

Homer: I'll have the smiley face breakfast special. Uhh, but could you add a bacon nose? Plus bacon hair, bacon mustache, five o'clock shadow made of bacon bits and a bacon body.

Waitress: How about I just shove a pig down your throat?

Waitress: I was kidding.

Homer: "Fine, but the bacon man lives in a bacon house!"

"You know that feeling you get when a thousand knives of fire are stabbing you in the heart? I'm having that right now… Ooh, bacon!"

"Special day! Oh, what have I forgotten now? Now, don't panic. Is it Bacon Day? No, that's crazy talk!"

"Let's see-Farmer Billy's smoke-fed bacon, Farmer Billy's bacon-fed bacon, Farmer Billy's travel bacon… Mr. Simpson, if you really want to kill yourself, I also sell handguns!" Apu, The Simpsons

"I'd be a vegetarian if bacon grew on trees…"

More TV Bacon Quotes

"Uh, "Hello, room service? I'd like some bacon, a couple of cokes, and a bunch of whores." Butthead, Beavis and ButtHead

"I'm never gonna get used to the 31st century. Caffeinated bacon? Baconated grapefruit?" Fry, Futurama

"I enjoy having breakfast in bed. I like waking up to the smell of bacon, sue me, and since I don't have a butler, I have to do it myself. So, most nights before I go to bed, I will lay six strips of bacon out on my George Foreman grill. Then I go to sleep. When I wake up, I plug in the grill. I go back to sleep again. Then I wake up to the smell of crackling bacon. It is delicious, it's good for me, it's the perfect way to start the day." Michael Scott – The Office

"Good Morning sweety. Oh my God, is that bacon? I love you, I love you, I love you." Grace – Will & Grace

"Why was there BACON IN THE SOAP? Zim, Invader Zim

Bacon Poetry

from 1915

Bat, bat,
Come under my hat,
And I'll give you a slice of bacon;
And when I bake
I'll give you a cake,
If I am not mistaken.

Below from web site Bacon Today

With words I cannot express
That without bacon we're under duress
Pork uniting us equally
With a love that's delightfully
Positive and exuberant
Bacon is a hate deterrent
Salty, crunchy and addicting
It's utterly delicious and uplifting
-Brianne Rivlin

Bacon, bacon on my mind
Will you give me a big behind?
No I say, this can't be true
Fatty pork is good for you
So when you walk that market aisle
A package of bacon should make you smile
Be not afraid of it on your plate
Your mood, you see, will elevate
Bacon. Bacon on my mind
In the fridge you are enshrined!
-*Russ Driver*

A pig's orgasm lasts thirty minutes.
(God's way of thanking them for bacon)

Three Legged Pig

One time I discovered a pig. It was a nice pig, as pigs go, but it only had three legs. The right back leg was wooden. I was as curious, so I asked the farmer, "Excuse me, sir. Why does your pig have a wooden leg?"

"Well, boy, that there is a courageous pig. The wife and I were asleep in the house one night, when that pig came running in and woke us up. The whole place was ablaze. We just got out alive."

"And the pig got its leg burned up in the fire?"

"Nope. Pig got out just fine. Matter of fact, he even went back in and saved the kids."

"Then why does the pig have a wooden leg?"

"I told you, boy. That is a brave pig. A heroic pig. That pig saved our lives."

"Yes, sir, but why does he have a wooden leg?"

"Boy, a pig like that, you don't eat all in one sitting."

ENDNOTES

Please celebrate International Bacon Day on the Saturday before Labor Day in the US, which is the first Monday in September.

Also, because bacon needs more than one holiday, December 30 is National Bacon Day. Do not pass on any of the local unofficial "bacon days" that are held by various organizations and communities. They are just expressing their bacon love and that is always a good thing.

* * *

Overdone Bacon - Now I know I must have crossed the line with so many bacon comments. This site page title from Grupthink is 'Mmmm. . . Bacon' and my 'Bloginalia 2010' book is posted with two other food books.
http://www.grupthink.com/answer/104422/Mmmmm_bacon

* * *

Bacon Obituary - August, 2014 - "Richard Norton Bacon (Rick) of Lumberton has left the building. His friends will tell you he's in a better place. The rest will say they can smell the Bacon burning. He is stress-free and at peace. The curtain came down on Thursday night at Southeastern Regional Medical Center." (legacy.com)

* * *

Making Machine-Gun Bacon with Ted Cruz

Here is an interesting video of 2016 presidential hopeful Ted Cruz cooking bacon with a machine gun.

https://www.youtube.com/watch?t=10&v=EaZGaJrd3x8

* * *

A 1993 YouTube of Christopher Walken reading "The Three Little Pigs."

https://www.youtube.com/watch?v=uWTwCuDbZ3E

* * *

There is a video with Hugh Jackman aka Wolverine singing about makin' bacon pancakes'. Copy or type the link into your browser.
https://www.youtube.com/watch?v=socABHT1Fjc

* * *

The following are a few folks that have been spectacularly wrong when they so brazenly declared the end of bacon.

Bacon Backlash - This not the first or last time the Wall Street Journal has been so wrong. From the Wall Street Journal, Katy McLaughlin, Oct. 2, 2010 - "We are in the midst of a bacon bubble and a growing number of chefs (some of whom quietly admit they helped inflate the bubble to begin with) say it's about to pop. Bacon had a good run, but now it has gone flabby, used too much and too often, it has lost its novelty and coated fine dining with a ubiquitous veneer of porky grease." *Sorry Katie, the bubble just keeps getting bigger and bacon will not pop. It just continues to sizzle.*

* * *

Bacon has Jumped the Shark - Back in 2007, Grub Street web site said we have gone too far. "But to say 'everything should taste like bacon', like the zealous producers of Bacon Salt do, is perhaps taking the obsession too far." "At the end of the day, as at the beginning, all we want from bacon is more of it. We can live without the accessories entirely." *Yes, the writers may be purists, but there is plenty of room for the rest of us bacon lovers - and we have yet to go far enough with bacon.*

* * *

Taco Bell: The Bacon Backlash Cometh - The sogoodblog, in 2009 predicted the end of bacon. "Like LOLcats, bacon is on the way out, friends." "I'm just sick of the saturation." "I demand we take back bacon by not mentioning it every five seconds when talking about food. In ten years time, bacon should then be under-appreciated, and we can all join together and start Bacon Fad 2.0 in 2019." *Sorry sogoodblog, it is still not the end of bacon. Many other things may come and go, but bacon just keeps coming.*

* * *

In May, 2009, The Seattle Stranger web site declared The end of baconmania and added our long coronary nightmare is almost over. *Oh, you are so wrong in Seattle.*

* * *

In December 2012, Josh Ozersky wrote in Time that, "Bacon as a trend is a monster that won't die, and I can't understand why." *He must be a bacon denier.*

* * *

Bacon is Dead - The J-Walk Blog, in 2008 declared "Bacon, You're Dead to Me. I never thought I'd say this, but I've had it with bacon. Let's be clear: I love bacon as much as the next person. I just can't understand the mass bacon worship cropping up in every restaurant, bar, and blog. I love waking up to the smell of it, but I don't need an alarm clock to cook it at my bedside. I love eating it next to a mound of warm, syrupy French toast, but I'm not interested in turning my breakfast into a miniature, perishable Stonehenge. The universe, or at least the culinary one, is obsessed with bacon lately. I may not be any kind of authority in the food world, but I am going to go out on a limb here and declare (or maybe just plead) that bacon is over. I agree. This is the final Bacon post at the J-Walk Blog." *From the number of comments posted, bacon is not dead and still enjoys growing porcine popularity.*

* * *

George Custer, later famous for his "last stand" in the Battle of Little Big Horn thirty years after the Civil War, ended up taking the table upon which the Civil War surrender document was signed. His widow, Elizabeth Bacon Custer.

* * *

Swine Flu - You are more likely to die from a coconut falling on your head than from Swine Flu - *Oh, I mean H1N1.* The US government and the World Health Organization are taking the 'swine' out of 'swine flu', but the experts who track the genetic heritage of the virus say, "If it is genetically mostly porcine and its parents are pig viruses, then it is swine flu." Six of the eight genetic segments of this virus strain are purely swine flu and the other two segments are bird and human.

Incidentally, The US government is ditching the swine label, because many people are afraid to eat pork and hurting the mega billion dollar US pork industry. The experts who point to the swine genetic origins of the virus agree that people cannot get the disease from food or handling pork, even raw. *Eat more bacon.*

They used to play rock, paper, scissors, bacon.
They took out the bacon because it always won.

The End

If you enjoyed this book, please tell your friends, Thanks!

Made in the USA
Coppell, TX
12 June 2021